THEY'RE OFF

THEY'RE OFF

AN AUTOBIOGRAPHY

JACK JARVIS

LONDON
MICHAEL JOSEPH

First published in Great Britain by
MICHAEL JOSEPH LTD
52 Bedford Square
London, W.C.1
1969

7181 0711 X

Printed in Great Britain by
Northumberland Press Limited
Gateshead

ILLUSTRATIONS

Thanks are due to *The British Racehorse* for
the photographs facing pages 32, 33, 64, 65, 80,
81, and 96; to Fox Photos for the photograph
facing page 73; to Photo Press (Leeds) for the
photograph facing page 97; to *The Cambridge
News* for the photograph facing page 128; to
Record House, Glasgow, for the photograph
facing page 129; and to Monitor Press Features
Ltd. for the photograph facing page 129.

FOREWORD

by The Earl of Rosebery

KT., PC., DSO., MC., LL.D., FRCSE., Bt.

In 1922 my father decided to move his racehorses to Newmarket as he was then an invalid and thought he might be able to see them better there. I was deputed to find him a trainer. I asked Jack Jarvis to take them and from that year until December 1968 when he died we had an uninterrupted association. We became great friends and during all those years never once did we have a serious disagreement.

Jarvis was a remarkable man and outstanding worker with a great sense of duty. Until his doctor stopped him he worked unceasingly for local activities, such as the Town Council etc. and this on top of his duties as a trainer, which most people would think would be ample employment without anything more.

During these 46 years he trained five classic winners and a Gold Cup winner for my father and myself, besides numerous other winners for other people.

He was a forthright and downright person who left people in no doubt as to what his view was and he was somewhat quick tempered. But that was soon over and if he antagonised anyone it was not long before they became friends again. He was respected by every section of the racing public and during all

7

these years there never was the slightest suspicion as to his integrity. He had great enthusiasm for everything he took up. I can vouch for the fact that he was a first class shot. At one time he was a most successful pigeon racer and he owned the winner of the Waterloo Cup.

Few people in his profession can have made and kept so many friends or got more out of life.

CHAPTER I

That horses and racing should dominate my life was inevitable.

My great-grandfather on my father's side of the family trained Gustavus who won the Derby in 1821, the first grey horse to become the winner of the 'Blue Riband'. Another of my predecessors used to do the catering on the racecourse at Newmarket, entries for overnight races being advertised to close at 'Jarvis's Booth'.

My father, William Jarvis, was a Newmarket trainer. The best horse he ever had under his care was undoubtedly Cyllene. Unfortunately for him, Cyllene, a very late foal, had been so small in his early days that it was thought pointless to enter him for the classics. He proved to be a top-class race-horse, far superior in fact to his contemporary Jeddah who won the 1898 Derby at 100/1. He won the Gold Cup at Ascot and subsequently sired four Derby winners—Cicero, Minoru, Lemberg and Tagalie. It was a great loss to British breeders when he was sold for £25,000 and exported to the Argentine at the comparatively early age of thirteen.

My father also trained a good horse in Ravensbury,

who, like Cyllene, belonged to Mr. C. D. Rose. It was Ravensbury's misfortune to be foaled the same year as that great horse Isinglass, and he was runner-up to Isinglass in the Two Thousand Guineas, the Derby and the St. Leger. In the Derby Ravensbury was ridden by Harry Barker, who ten weeks previously had finished second in the Grand National on Aesop.

Ravensbury undoubtedly won the Grand Prix de Paris at Longchamp, but in the eighteen nineties the English were anything but popular in France and when the crowd saw that Ravensbury had won, there was a tremendous outburst of booing. However the judge, doubtless from motives of the highest patriotism, proceeded to award the verdict to the French horse Rogotsky, the runner-up, whereupon there were deafening cheers and hats were thrown into the air. What Messrs. Weatherby thought of the incident is shown in the Racing Calendar which gives the result as won by 'a very short head', this being to the best of my belief the only occasion this term has been used in the history of 'Races Past'.

My father obtained some compensation a few years later when he took his great hurdler Karakoul to France and won the big hurdle race at Auteuil. Karakoul was probably one of the best hurdlers of all time and a race named after him used to be run at Hurst Park, the scene of his triumph over Mark Time in a famous Match. Incidentally Ravensbury, for all his bad luck, won several good races including the Ascot Stakes, the Hardwicke Stakes, and the Manchester November Handicap with 9st. 4 on his back.

My mother's father, James Godding, trained Macaroni, who won the Derby for Mr. R. C. Naylor in

1863. It was a very dry summer in Macaroni's year and most of the Newmarket trainers with Derby candidates took them to the Wiltshire Downs where the going was alleged to be better. However Godding firmly refused to leave Newmarket, saying that if he could not train on the Limekilns, he could not train anywhere. When Macaroni won, there were great rejoicings at Newmarket and the bells of All Saints Church were rung, for it was believed with some justification that Godding's action had saved Newmarket as the main centre of training in England.

Godding trained at Palace House which he owned and later sold to the Rothschild family, who for some years rented it to me. It was there I kept the horses that I had not room for at Park Lodge. Among Godding's patrons at Palace House was that eccentric and fiery-tempered old aristocrat Lord Glasgow. Going round the stables one evening Godding, accompanied by Lord Glasgow, came to an exceptionally good looking horse that Lord Glasgow admired very much. At this juncture Godding unfortunately thought he would be funny and remarked, 'Believe it or not, my lord, but this horse's owner only lives eight miles away, but has never seen him.' Lord Glasgow replied that if only he himself owned a horse like that, he would travel a hundred miles to see it. 'Yes,' said Godding, preparing for the laugh, 'but the owner in question happens to be blind.' Old Lord Glasgow was furious; he picked up a fork, chased Godding out of the box and removed all his horses the very next day.

My eldest brother Willie succeeded Richard Marsh as trainer to King George V, for whom he won the One Thousand Guineas with Scuttle, while my other brother, Basil, was also a successful trainer and won the Derby with Papyrus in 1923. I shall have something to say later on of Papyrus's famous trip to America to run in a Match against Zev. From early childhood I heard endless talk of horses and racing and long before I was ten I knew that a curb on the pavement was better than one on the horse's hock. I learnt to ride so early in my life that I just cannot remember it at all. It is hardly surprising that my first ambition was to be a jockey. When playing about I used to practise picking up my whip and could very soon twist it round my fingers without fear of dropping it. Perhaps for that reason I hold the view that for a jockey to drop his whip or to fumble when picking it up is unforgivable. My father taught me many things about horses and race-riding, urging me above all to keep my hands down and never look round. It makes me shudder to see the way some modern jockeys turn round in the saddle and unbalance their mounts.

When I was eleven I joined my two brothers at Cranleigh School in Surrey, but I was always worrying my parents to let me leave and get on with my riding. In the end, when my brothers left, I was allowed to leave, too. Willie then went to be assistant to my uncle, James Ryan, at Green Lodge, where he held the post of private trainer to Mr. J. H. Houldsworth, surely one of the finest sportsmen ever to own horses. Mr. Houldsworth only wanted to race at the best meetings and he hated handicaps on the grounds that they encouraged cheating. He was not in the least pleased when his horse Balsarroch won the Cesarewitch and in fact only permitted him to compete to please my uncle.

My brother Basil and I finished our education with a tutor. Basil rode one or two winners but soon got too heavy. For a time he used to travel with my father's horses to meetings away from Newmarket and then took up training on his own account. We had been blessed with wonderful parents. My mother was devoted to her three sons and I am sure that both she and my father denied themselves much in the early days for the sake of their children. My father, though, was not the man to tolerate any form of slackness. I had to start right from the bottom by 'doing my two', in other words looking after a couple of horses. Each morning I was up early, made one of my horses ready and rode out to exercise; on return I dressed it over, fed it and let it loose for the day. Then came breakfast followed by the same routine with the other horse, all of which took me to well after one o'clock. In the evening I had to spend a full hour at each horse, strapping them both thoroughly. My father went round stables in the evening and could be very sarcastic to any lad if he found a mane dusty or feet improperly greased. He was a first-class stableman and a great judge of a horse. What I learned from him has been of incalculable value to me throughout my life. Not the least important advice he passed on to me was Admiral Rous's old dictum 'to keep yourself in the best company and your horses in the worst'.

In July came a red-letter day in my life; I had my first ride in a race. As long as I live I shall never forget the excitement of that day. I was to partner a horse called Black Friar in a race at Newmarket run over the July Course. The morning dragged on and I was

13

down on the course at least an hour and a half before the first event on the card was due to be run. Although my mount was reckoned to have no chance, it seemed to me I might possibly win. I cantered down to the post in a dream. The gate went up and we were 'off'. There was what appeared to me a mad rush and it was soon all over, Black Friar and I finishing unplaced somewhere about the middle of the field. Nevertheless, I managed to learn quite a lot, how to weigh in and out, how to take my place at the start, and above all that no boy, however promising, can be expected to do himself justice until he has had several rides and got over the strangeness of it all. I invariably keep an old horse and enter him in all the apprentice races at Newmarket. Although he never has a chance of winning, he gives my boys valuable experience before I put them up on something that has a genuine prospect of success.

All this, by the way, reminds me of a letter I once received. I had a horse called Brabazon which we used as a hack. In addition I used him in all the apprentice races at Newmarket to give my boys a ride. This procedure had continued for several seasons. Now one day I opened a letter from a man I had never heard of who said he was a follower of my stable and had many good wins on my horses; 'but', he went on, 'there is one horse I would like to draw your attention to—Brabazon. I can only think that you would not keep running him unless you hoped to bring off a coup'. I really felt rather sorry for the writer so I sent him a letter explaining the true situation.

I cannot pretend to remember my next few rides

but at the start of the following season I went up to Lincoln and rode a horse of my father's called Ray that finished second. After that second race a man whom I did not know came up to me in the weighing room and asked me if I could ride in the Earl of Sefton's Plate at Liverpool later that week. Of course I accepted with alacrity. He then told me that the horse I was to ride was The Page and that it stood a very good chance. That stranger turned out to be Billy Higgs, later to become a very successful jockey. He had been sent over from Ireland by his employer, Mr. J. C. Sullivan, to engage a light-weight to ride The Page at Liverpool. He had been impressed by the way I had ridden Ray and I have always thought what remarkable confidence he must have had in his own judgment to engage a boy who had never ridden a winner. I duly went to Liverpool and beat the great Danny Maher, who was riding a good horse of Lord Stanley's called Pellisson, by a head. I still retain vivid memories of that race. Six furlongs round the turn at Liverpool is a pretty good test for a boy. I got well away and kept The Page on the rails. Danny came at me at the distance but in a tremendous finish our light weight told and we held on to win by a matter of inches.

This was a wonderful start for a boy, particularly as I got a very good press. I began to get quite a lot of rides from outside my father's stable. In fact it was this victory on The Page that really launched my career on the Turf, a career that was to last for well over half a century and bring me into contact with people famous not merely in racing circles, but in the history of England, too.

CHAPTER II

My next winner was at the First Spring Meeting at
Newmarket when I rode Archon, one of the horses I
used to 'do' in my father's stable. I won by a head
from a horse ridden by Billy Griggs and trained by
Bob Sherwood, to whom Griggs was apprenticed.
Sherwood was very much inclined to blame his jockey
if things went wrong, and until he got tired of me as
well, he took Billy Griggs off and put me up on the
stable light-weights. I was now getting pretty well
established and by the end of the season I had ridden
thirty-five winners, including Hacklers Pride in the
Cambridgeshire. The story of that Cambridgeshire is
worth recording as one of the biggest coups ever
known on the Turf was successfully landed.

Hacklers Pride was a three-year-old filly handi-
capped at 7st. 1, and as I claimed the 5lb. allowance
she actually carried 6st. 10. She was owned by Captain Frank Forester, a famous Master of the Quorn,
and was trained by Jack Fallon at Druids Lodge, a
few miles from Netheravon. Druids Lodge was then
run by a syndicate of very shrewd owners of whom
Captain W. B. Purefoy, Mr. A. P. Cunliffe and Captain Forester were the leading lights. It was generally

accepted, though, that Captain Purefoy was the cleverest member of what was known to the racing public as 'the Druids Lodge Confederacy'. They had already hit the ring very hard on several occasions and in the spring of this particular year they had brought off a spectacular gamble when Ypsilanti won the Jubilee, a performance they were to repeat with equal success with the same horse twelve months later. Hacklers Pride, incidentally, won the Cambridgeshire the following year as well, while Christmas Daisy won a stack of money for the 'confederacy' by winning the Cambridgeshire in 1909 and 1910.

Plans for the coup were carefully laid. Hacklers Pride was a very hard puller so the first problem was to find a boy that could hold her. I was engaged to ride her in the six furlong Stewards Cup at Goodwood. I was told nothing and I had no trouble in holding her down to the post. It was a dreadful afternoon with rain pouring down and visibility so bad that racing nearly had to be abandoned. I finished somewhere in the middle of the field and after the race my father saw the lad who 'did' Hacklers Pride trying to put her rug on, but having difficulty in the wind and rain. He gave the lad a helping hand whereupon the lad observed in a broad Irish accent: 'Let your little boy ride this one again; she hasn't done a canter for a month.' The following week my father was asked to let the Druids Lodge stable have a second claim on my services for the rest of the season. We found out afterwards that this was done solely to secure me for the Cambridgeshire and in fact I only rode once more for them before that race.

In those days the ante-post market was much

17

stronger than it is today. Druids Lodge had several horses entered for the Cambridgeshire including Ypsilanti and a three-year-old called Uninsured that won the Lincoln the following spring. Both of these were in turn favourite, or nearly so, during the weeks prior to the race. Suddenly, with only a few days to go, the stable commission was launched, not only in England, but in Australia, South Africa and every country where bets on the Cambridgeshire were accepted. Within a few hours the 'confederacy' had backed Hacklers Pride to win a quarter of a million pounds.

When I walked out to the parade ring I was still unaware that Hacklers Pride was a racing certainty. The first thing that happened was that my whip was taken away from me. 'You won't need that, Sonny, she is a free goer so just ride her out with your hands.' I was then informed that the ankle boots she was wearing because of the danger of hitting herself through her tremendous hind action would be taken off down at the start, her lad having been sent on in advance for that purpose. Everything was going smoothly according to plan, but then something happened which very nearly wrecked the whole scheme. The supremely fit filly that Hacklers Pride was on Cambridgeshire day represented a very different proposition from what she had been at Goodwood.

When I was let go to canter down to the post, away she went and I simply could not hold one side of her. For a few dreadful moments we looked like galloping to Cambridge, taking the stable money with us. Luckily, however, the planning came to the rescue. The lad that had been sent down to the post had just reached the seven furlong starting gate when he saw his filly approaching, obviously out of control. With considerable presence of mind he ran out on to the course and shouted at her. She recognised his voice and eased up just sufficiently for me to get a pull at her. I pulled her round in a circle—luckily there is plenty of room at Newmarket—and as she came by the lad again he grabbed her and led her the rest of the way to the start. When the gate went up I was one of the first away, and after a hundred yards I never saw another horse in the race. My reward was £125, not very liberal in view of what the stable had won, but very nice for a boy of fifteen in those days. I hope they treated that lad with the generosity he so richly deserved.

In all I rode one hundred and twenty-one winners on the flat and two over jumps. Among the notable winners I rode were Wet Paint in the Prince Edward Handicap at Manchester, Kilglass in the Ayr Gold Cup and Romer in the Derby Cup. Unfortunately increasing weight was soon to cut short my career as a jockey. While I was out walking one day to try and get off a pound or two, a brougham drove up behind me and out stepped Mrs. Langtry, 'The Jersey Lily', who was then living at Kentford, about four miles from Newmarket.

'Don't stop for me,' she said, 'I can walk as well as you can and I'm going to walk back to Newmarket with you.' Telling her coachman to follow on behind, she proceeded to accompany me into Newmarket, doing a fair heel and toe and chatting ceaselessly the whole way. We soon discovered we were both on the same diet trying to reduce our weight. At this period she was an oldish woman and confided to me that although she did not mind becoming grey and wrinkled, she had a horror of getting fat. Pointing to the belt she was wearing, she demonstrated how she had been able to take it in three holes since she started her diet. She was a remarkable woman for her age, full of vivacity and energy.

On one occasion my father and I were staying at Folkestone for the races. As we entered our compartment in the special train for Westernhanger, in climbed Lily Langtry—she was actually Lady de Bathe then—and her entourage. She was acting in a play at Folkestone at the time. Just as the train was pulling out, a policeman put his head in at the window and said, 'Be careful the other end, m'Lady, "The Boys" are after your jewellery.'

This caused a certain amount of consternation in the carriage, one of the old-fashioned sort without a corridor, and a discussion took place on what was the best thing to do. In the end a crocodile-skin jewel case which she had with her was handed over to me. When the train pulled into the racecourse siding, I put it under my arm with my macintosh over it, walked straight through and handed it over to the Clerk of the Course. 'The Boys' had been buzzing round the door of our compartment like flies, but they knew me well by sight and took no notice of me. I often wonder if they ever discovered how they had been outwitted. It was Lady de Bathe, by the way, who gave Fred Darling his start as a trainer. Fred had a jumper or two in his stable at Kentford and I used to ride them for him. I was nearly killed riding one of them, Shy Lad, at Windsor. I took a really bad fall and was in bed for several weeks with severe concussion.

It was with a hurdler that I managed to get hold of my first real money. I saw a gelding trained by Dick Marsh run at Doncaster and it struck me he was just the type to make a useful jumper. He was ridden by Henri Jelliss who was just a small boy at the time. I travelled home in the same compartment as Jelliss who told me that he would undoubtedly have won had he been able to hold the horse. When I got home I did my best to persuade my father to buy the horse, and a few days later, as we were riding together on the Heath, I saw Dick Marsh watching his horses work. My father went up to him and asked him if by chance he had a horse that might make a jumper for me. Marsh said that he had and mentioned the horse I had seen run at Doncaster, a three-year-old by Florizel II out of Pitcroy. The price was £400 and it was agreed that I was to go over and look at the horse, and if I liked him, I was to have him. I took our pony trap, a spare boy, a saddle and bridle and a cheque for £400, returning home with the horse shortly afterwards.

A few days later I gave him his first school and he proved to be a natural jumper. I named him Pitsea but unfortunately, before I could run him, he threw out a large thoropin. Because of this it was some time before I could really get on with him. However I got him right and put him in the £1000 Liverpool Hurdle. I rode him myself and although there was a big field and it was his first effort in public over hurdles, he won in a canter, making a pretty big impression on all who saw him. He had had to run, of course, in my father's name.

21

After the race I put on my coat and went to see if Pitsea was all right. On the way I ran into Aubrey Hastings, then one of the leading National Hunt trainers and father of the late Peter Hastings-Bass who trained at Kingsclere. Hastings asked me if my father was prepared to sell Pitsea as Prince Hatzfeld, who won the 1906 Grand National with Ascetic's Silver ridden by Hastings himself, wanted to buy him. I said the price was £4000, a pretty stiff one for a jumper in those days. Hastings went off and fetched the Prince and together they had a good look at Pitsea. The Prince said it was a lot of money—which was perfectly true—and he would like to think about it. 'He'll have it,' whispered Hastings to me.

On the way back to the paddock we met my father wearing a satisfied grin on his face. He pulled me aside and the following little conversation took place:

'I've just sold the horse,' said my father.

'What?' I replied dumbfounded, 'sold the horse? How much for?'

'For £3,000 to Mr. Prentice and he will stay in the stable.'

'Good gracious,' I said, or words to that effect, 'I have just sold him for £4,000.'

Of course the sale to Mr. Prentice had to stand. A few weeks later I was beaten a head on Pitsea in the Jubilee Hurdle at Manchester. Lester Piggott's grandfather, Ernie Piggott, rode the winner. He was a beautiful horseman and I think could have won on either of them.

It was at that same Liverpool meeting that I rode my last winner on the flat, a mare called Easter, who was very bad at the gate and had been getting herself left. There was a mile and a half selling race, amateur riders, jockeys 6lbs. extra, and as I could do the weight my father entered the mare. I had been going down to the post with her trying to get her to start and Mr. Willoughby, the Starter, knew her well and was very helpful. I told him before the race that as long as I was straight I did not mind losing a length or so. I stood behind and when they were straight I came in on the move. I was a couple of lengths behind the others, but as the gate went up I gave her a couple of hot ones with the whip and in fact we lost very little ground. She won the race all right from some horse ridden by Danny Maher. I had therefore won my first and my last flat-race at Liverpool, beating Danny Maher on each occasion.

At this period I was retained as first jockey by Mr. A. Stedall who had a lot of horses in training with Alf Sadler. Another patron of the stable was Sir Henry Randall, whose son Bert used to ride his horses. One day at Brighton each owner was running a horse in the same race. In the parade ring Alf beckoned to me and Bert and said, 'Now, boys, both on your merits, and if they run up to their trial they will run a dead-heat.' Which they then proceeded to do.

Mr. Stedall owned a very moderate horse called Leopold. Now it so happened that Leopold was entered for the 1905 Derby and Mr. Stedall thought he would like to see his colours carried in that great race. In those days the crowd used to throng on to the course at Epsom between races and the mounted police had to clear the track before the following event. As soon as the horses were round Tattenham Corner, out would come the crowd again to watch them going away to the winning post up the straight. Leopold and I were unlucky; the crowd ran out before we arrived.

Mr. Stedall was a great port drinker and anywhere he stayed regularly he used to keep a store of vintage port. He did this at Freemason Lodge where Alf Sadler trained. One night at dinner his port was borne in by a new maid. 'Have you shaken it?' Mr. Stedall asked anxiously. 'No,' replied the maid, 'but I can,' and proceeded to do so.

The best winner I ever rode for Mr. Stedall was Marsden in what was an important handicap in those days, the Peveril of the Peak at Derby. I remember about this time playing in a charity cricket match at the Oval, Jockeys *v* Champion Amateur Athletes. I bought a nice new bat for the occasion from Bobby Abel, but it did not get very much use as I was middle man in a hat-trick brought off by Alfred Shrubb, one of the greatest runners of his day.

Before leaving my riding career for good, I should like to recall a little incident one winter day at Lingfield. There was a tough old jockey called Tommy Dunn who would ride anything for three quid and knew every move in the game. He and I both fell at that hurdle on the top of the hill at the furthest point from the stands. As I was picking myself up he shouted to me, 'Lay still, you bloody fool, and they will send the ambulance for us!'

CHAPTER III

After giving up race-riding, or rather after it had given me up, I helped my father at Waterwitch House, taking my brother Basil's place as Travelling Head Man, Basil having started to train on his own account. I often wonder what some of the present day jockeys and trainers would think if they had to do the sort of travelling that we did in my young days. I remember several times my father and me catching the 6.30 a.m. 'Horse Special' from Newmarket to Haydock Park, which got the second day's runners there just before the first race. If we had no runners the second day, we would take a cab to Newton-Le-Willows after racing and catch the London train. From London we took a train which landed us at Cambridge somewhere about midnight. We finished our outing by carriage and pair, arriving at Newmarket at roughly 1.30 a.m. Not a bad day's work in my opinion, but hardly Trade Union hours.

I was a pretty good judge of form and managed to win quite a bit at betting. One day Mr. John Wood, who acted as Racing Manager to Mr. Leopold de Rothschild, came up to me and said, 'Is it true you have been winning some money?' When I admitted this was so, he went on : 'They were talking about you at dinner last night and Mr. de Rothschild told me to come and tell you to "put a nail through it" and if you liked, he would invest it for you.' I felt highly honoured to be recipient of kindly advice of the greatest financier of the day and I sent all I could spare to him at New Court, St. Swithins Lane. When World War I broke out, I placed the account in my wife's name and she continued to hold the investments for the rest of her life.

I was very anxious in the meantime to start up on my own as a trainer and was always on the lookout for an opportunity to do so. One day my aunt, Mrs. Ryan, told me she had heard from John Dawson, the trainer, that a certain Mr. Barton had leased Warren House, a big training establishment. That could only mean that he was setting up a private trainer there and it seemed to me just the chance that I had been looking for. At the very next Newmarket meeting the winner of a selling race was being sold and I found myself standing next to Mr. Barton. He made some comment to me about the animal being auctioned and this gave me the opening I needed. As we walked away from the sale ring I asked him if by chance he needed a private trainer for Warren House. He replied that he did not, but on the other hand he did know someone who was looking for a trainer and he was prepared to recommend me. He asked me a lot of questions about myself and some weeks later I received a telegram asking me to meet him at The Rutland Hotel for lunch. The upshot was that I was engaged as his private trainer, the terms being £300 a year, a house, coal and light, and the

26

choice of either the odds to £5 a winner or 10% of winning stakes. I chose the former, as with the type of animal owned by Mr. Barton, stake money was unlikely to be high, but on the other hand I felt I could probably place his horses to win in their proper class. I was to say nothing about the agreement, but was to be prepared to take over the horses early in January 1914.

I was delighted to get a start and although the salary could hardly be described as princely, I felt confident that I could make good. One question that Mr. Barton had asked with some concern was whether I was married. When he learnt that I was single, he said it was a pity as Warren House was a very big house and he wanted to retain a flat in it for race-weeks. If I had had a wife, she could have kept an eye on it for him, and he and his wife would have brought their own servants down when racing was on. I soon settled that little problem by saying that I could get married at once as my fiancée and I had been engaged for some time and had only been waiting for me to find a job.

As soon as I left Mr. Barton I dashed up to Wroughton House to tell Ethel Leader the great news. She was a daughter of Tom Leader who had trained George Frederick to win the Derby, and her brothers, Tom, Coll, Fred and Harvey were all trainers. We had been sweethearts as children at school together, were very much in love and remained so for the whole of our long and outstandingly happy married life. Many happy days we spent together with our daughter Vivien, travelling thousands of miles to South Africa, Japan, Australia, New Zealand

and South America, making many good friends in doing so. I have seen racing in many foreign countries and remain strongly of the opinion that taking everything into consideration, racing in England is the best.

Suddenly one day I had an urgent telephone call from Mr. Barton who told me he had had a row with his trainer and that I was to take over the horses at once. This was a bit of a problem as Warren House was not ready, the stables were in the hands of the painters, and I possessed neither staff nor saddlery. This I pointed out to Mr. Barton but he insisted that somehow or other I had got to take charge at once and the question of expense did not matter. I then remembered that Charles Archer was living in Ellesmere House and his stables were empty. I called on him and he consented to let me have the stables for one month, at a very high rent I might add. I borrowed some lads from my father and I engaged as Head Man a certain Percy Double on whom I had had my eye on for some time and who was then acting as a sort of minor Head Man for Bob Sherwood. I called on Sherwood and told him the position; very kindly he said he was only too delighted if I could give Double a better job and furthermore that I could have him right away. Double turned out to be the best Head Man any trainer ever had and he stayed with me until he died during the last war, having proved a wonderful servant and friend. Together we set to work with frenzied haste, while Gilbert, the saddler, and his staff worked overtime turning out rugs and equipment. With borrowed lads and saddlery we collected forty horses, some of which had to be put in the uncompleted boxes at Warren House as there was not room for them all at Ellesmere House. I think that was quite the most hectic day of my life. Starting with nothing, I took over forty horses and got them all out at exercise the following morning.

My first season as a trainer started well as I won two races the very first week, one at Lincoln, the other at Liverpool. At Lincoln I had my first winner with a sweet little filly called Symptoms, who stood only just 14.2. She went on and carried her penalty to victory at Harpenden, ridden by Fred Rickaby, father of Bill Rickaby who rode so many good winners for me in the years to come. Poor Fred was killed in action while serving in the Tank Corps. He was a beautiful jockey and won the One Thousand Guineas four times in five years. He and Fred Winter were great friends and it has been a great pleasure to see the sons of both of them doing so well as jockeys.

Altogether I had a very satisfactory season and Mr. Barton won a lot of money betting, which was his main objective. The best win we had was with a colt called My Ronald, a lovely dark brown horse by Dark Ronald. He had run a very high temperature the day after I took him over and as he looked the best of the lot, this was a bit of a shock to me. He soon recovered, but I gave him plenty of time before I really got on with him. War in fact had broken out before he had run. We decided to give him a race at Newmarket, not that he was really ready, but a race would bring him on more than several gallops and in any case we never knew for how long racing would be allowed to carry on.

I had a grand old jockey, 'Daddy' Spear, riding for me; he was a fine judge and would not have told his own mother about the chance of any of the horses he was riding. They were quite a good lot of two-year-olds running against My Ronald; I picked out a couple that had shown some good form and told 'Daddy' to see how near he could get to them without giving the colt a hard race. I also told him to get the colt into the middle of the field to teach him his business. After the race Spear informed me that My Ronald had given him a good feel and that he could have finished in front of one of the two I had picked out and that in fact had ended up fifth. Knowing the race would have brought My Ronald on, we were very pleased.

That night Mr. Barton and I discussed where we would run My Ronald next. I said there was a selling race at Alexandra Park closing on the following Tuesday and that he was sure to be a certainty for that. Mr. Barton feared we might lose him, but I pointed out that owing to the war few people were keen to buy horses. In any case if he had a good bet, he could afford to spend a bit to buy him in. Mr. Barton then rang up a man called Paddy Lyons and asked him how much he could get on S.P. at Alexandra Park without the money getting back. Lyons reckoned £500 was the limit. 'Not enough,' replied Mr. Barton, and eventually it was agreed that Lyons should be given the name of the horse three days before the race and that he would get £1,000 on.

Before the race Mr. Barton was worried about getting his horse back, but I assured him that if he did what I said, everything would turn out all right.

The selling ring at Alexandra Park is below the Members' Enclosure. I told Mr. Barton to stand where everyone could see him bid up to £300 and then to shake his head and walk away. I then got hold of old Johnny Hallick, the Lambourn trainer, who was a friend of mine, and as he had a bet on every race, no one would take much notice of him. I told Johnny to have a tenner on mine and then to buy him in for us after the race. I instructed him to bid against Mr. Barton if he happened to see Mr. Barton bidding and to go on bidding himself till I told him to stop.

My Ronald was a particularly nice looking two-year-old so I kept him in the stables for as long as I could so that no one could see him and only brought him into the parade ring at the last possible moment. The authorities were less particular about that sort of thing in those days. Old Spear rode a lovely race and won cleverly. When My Ronald came into the sale ring de Mestre, the Australian trainer, Mr. Barton and Hallick all joined in the bidding. At £300 Mr. Barton, who had been standing in the Members where all could see him, dropped out. De Mestre put in a few more bids and then he gave up, too, the horse being knocked down to Hallick. 'Bought In,' said Hallick to the auctioneer. 'Well I'm damned,' observed de Mestre. 'I knew that Barton would never part with anything good and when I saw him stop bidding I thought there must be something wrong with the horse.'

We next took My Ronald up to Leicester for a maiden race in which he carried a 7lb. penalty that brought his weight up to 9st. 7. He beat a colt trained by Dick Wootton, Stanley Wootton's father, and as Dick Wootton had his betting boots on, he made a good market for us.

The following season My Ronald did us even better. His first race was a mile handicap at Newbury. About ten days before the race I tried him with several other horses including Berildon, a six-year-old that had won the Lincoln two years previously. Ridden by Walter Earl, My Ronald won the gallop with the utmost ease. Riding home on our hacks I said to Walter 'This will be a certainty at Newbury.' 'Too good to be true,' he replied. My answer to that was that it was quite pointless trying a horse if you did not believe what you saw.

When we got to Newbury I found My Ronald was No. 21 on the card so I promptly doubled my bet. I must explain that I have always been superstitious about 21 ever since I was a jockey and rode five winners in the first week of the season, including the winner of the Liverpool Spring Cup, and every single one was No. 21 on the card. Later on I won the same race at Newbury with Lord Rosebery's Dunottar; he, too, was No. 21 and once more I doubled my bet. My Ronald duly won his Newbury race, beating a horse of Lord Durham's called Lux that had been heavily backed so once again we got a good price. It was an odd thing, but whenever My Ronald won, we nearly always seemed to find something well fancied to beat us and to make the market for us.

With the war dragging on, Mr. Barton decided to sell all his horses and this led to a transaction which would certainly have made a vast difference to the English Stud Book if it had come off.

32

J. Jarvis, rider of Hackler's Pride.

A photograph of me in the *Sporting and Dramatic* just
before I won the Cambridgeshire on Hacklers Pride.

Golden Myth—the horse that established my reputation—winner of the Queens Prize, Gold Vase, Gold Cup and Eclipse Stakes.

A man named Sol Goldhill asked me if I would advise him about buying some of Mr. Barton's horses for Australia. The upshot was that he bought three and engaged my Head Man, Percy Double, to take them to Australia, where they were destined for Sol Green, one of the leading owners over there. These three horses did well and some time later I received a letter from Sol Green asking me to buy a good horse for stud purposes and stating that a big price would be paid for the right article.

I sent out the names of several horses including that of Phalaris, who was winning some good races at the time. I then got a cable asking the price so I went along to Mr. Lambton, who trained Phalaris, and secured the offer at a very reasonable sum. I thought the deal as good as settled until I received another cable turning it down. I was naturally disappointed at the time but was later to realise how lucky for me the refusal had been, as without Phalaris there would have been no Fairway, and I have been exceptionally fortunate with Fairway's descendants —Blue Peter, Ocean Swell, and Honeyway to name only three. When Percy Double came back to work for me again after the war, he said Sol Green had turned down Phalaris on the grounds that he would only sire sprinters.

CHAPTER IV

After the war, as soon as I was demobilised—I had been attached to the Tank Corps as a sergeant instructor in communications—I had to set about making an entirely fresh start. At that time Park Lodge, where I now train, was occupied by troops. Many famous trainers had had their horses there, including Bob Sherwood, Charles Waugh, Reg Day, Jack Brewer and the Hon. Francis Lambton, the last named of whom had been training there up till the war when he went to the front and was killed. The actual owner of Park Lodge was Mrs. Barrett, widow of George Barrett, a leading jockey in the late Victorian era. She agreed to let it to me on a yearly tenancy, knowing that by so doing she would be assisted in regaining possession. My father said I was mad to take such a big place without any horses and if I did not get any in pretty quick time, I should soon be broke. I replied that if I didn't get any horses to train I should be broke anyway and having Park Lodge would merely accelerate the process. As it was, at least I should have a stable to put the horses in if anyone offered me any.

When I actually moved into Park Lodge I had

34

precisely three horses. One of these three was Star-flower, owned by a very old friend named Jerry Cripps, a great-hearted man who was loved by all who knew him, especially his fellow members at the Eccentric Club. He had bought this horse solely to give me a start. The second horse was owned by a friend of his called Rawson, and the third was a little filly I had bought from a farmer for £30. It was this little £30 animal which did most to get me started again. I put her in a seller at Birmingham, knowing that horses were in short supply after the war and almost anything that could walk was capable of winning a selling race. The most fancied horse was Vandy Beatty's The Wrecker, who had been bought-in not long before for a quite big price after winning a selling hurdle. Just before the start Sam Pickering remarked to me 'It will be all right for you if you can manage to be second to The Wrecker.' In the end an animal trained by Bert Lines beat The Wrecker a head and I was third. Directly after the race a man called Bob Tilly came up to me and offered me £500 to claim The Wrecker as by the rules then in force I was entitled to first claim. Then up came Vandy Beatty and he suggested that we should 'claim friendly', in other words each claim the other's horse but in fact retain our own. To this I replied that I should be delighted if someone claimed mine, but that I had been offered £500 profit on his! However, as I did not like claiming horses, he could have his back for £50. I was under the impression that I was being extremely generous in doing myself out of £450 that I could ill afford. Beatty, however, appeared to take a somewhat different view and asked me to oblige as a friend; as he never by any chance spoke to me, I did not really see the point of that remark and closed the conversation by saying I had decided to keep the horse.

Presently Sir William Cooke came to me and said he heard I had claimed The Wrecker and that the horse's owner, Captain Davy, wanted it back. I explained what had transpired with The Wrecker's trainer so he then took me along and introduced me to Captain Davy, who, he assured me, would consider I had acted very fairly. Captain Davy was very nice about it and agreed to my offer; not so Beatty, however, who remarked in very hostile fashion 'I'll get even with you.' To this I replied, 'I'll start now and keep the horse.'

This put the cat among the pigeons. Back came Sir William Cooke and Captain Davy. I said if there was going to be ill-feeling I might as well have it for £500 rather than £50. However Sir William Cooke, who had been a friend of my father's, persuaded me in the end to accept the £50. Good was to come of this rather unpleasant little incident as later on Sir William sent me some of his horses to train because 'I had obliged him over the matter'. The following year I got all his horses including Golden Orb who won the Wokingham Stakes at 7/4, my first Ascot winner, and Devizes, who won the Doncaster Cup and many other good races. I trained a lot of winners for Sir William and when eventually he left me to have his horses trained on his own property he gave me as a parting present a lovely old cup with all the performances of Devizes engraved on it.

I have never been a heavy bettor, but I admit that

I went for a very big win with Devizes in the Cesare-witch. Sir William and I both backed him at long odds and on the day I stood to win more money than ever before or since. He was a delightful horse to train and before a race he would play about, giving little buck jumps, while when his rugs were removed he used to let fly with both legs. Before this particular race he walked round very quietly and this worried me as I felt that in my anxiety to have him fit for the most exacting race of the season, I might have given him just one gallop too many.

I had a boy waiting with my hack by the paddock gate and I cantered down to the Ditch Gap to watch the early stages of the race. I then turned round and galloped over to join them at the entrance to the rails. I was a bit disappointed to see Spear, who rode Devizes, having to niggle at him to keep his place, but when Devizes struck the front at the Bushes I really thought he was going to win. He faded out, though, in the final furlong and finished about 5th or 6th.

I could not see Spear when I got back to the pad-dock, but Tommy Robins, who had been riding in the race, told me he knew Devizes had 'gone' before the start as the horse had been coughing all the way down. Later on Spear confirmed this and said but for the big bets at stake he would certainly have brought the horse back. The odd thing is that Devizes never coughed once in the paddock before he went down to the start. That night he had a temperature of 104. His subsequent form—he was second in the Ascot Stakes with 9st. 7—indicates that he really was a certainty.

About the same time that I took over Sir William

Cooke's horses, Sir George Bullough, who up till then had only owned jumpers, decided he would go in for flat racing. He had wanted Frank Barling to train his horses, but as Barling was training privately for Lord Glanely, he advised Sir George to send them to me. Sir George accordingly asked me to buy him some yearlings. The first one I bought was a colt by Tredennis out of Golden Lily, a mare by Persimmon. He was named Golden Myth and he proved to be the horse that really put me on the map as a trainer. Moreover he did much the same for Charlie Elliott as a jockey. I have been wonderfully lucky with the first horse that I have bought for various owners, but I will have more to say on this later on.

As a two year old Golden Myth was big and backward and we never ran him. At three years of age he won first time out at Nottingham, a maiden race which we very nearly lost owing to a bit of combined carelessness on the part of the Clerk of the Scales and myself. It was a race in which apprentices were allowed 3lbs., those that had never ridden a winner an additional 3lbs., making 6lbs. in all. Charlie Elliott, who was apprenticed to me, was to ride and in the previous race he was to ride a colt called Rakings. Both were to carry the same weight so I told Charlie just to change his colours and use the same saddle and weight cloth. Charlie then proceeded to win on Rakings and I weighed him out for Golden Myth claiming the 6lbs., forgetting that by virtue of of his win he was now only entitled to claim three. I saddled Golden Myth and he took him into the parade ring. A well-known journalist called Archie Falcon beckoned to me, and not knowing what on earth he wanted to talk to me about, I walked over to the rails to where he was standing. He said 'Is this the same boy riding your horse that rode the last winner?' I said 'Yes.' 'Are you carrying the right weight?' he then asked. 'No,' I replied, and off I went, moving faster than I had ever moved before in my life. I got the saddle off and into the weighing room and weighed the boy out correctly. He won all right, by a neck. After the race I congratulated him on riding a good race, to which he replied 'Thank you, Sir, the other kid rode well, too.' The 'other kid' was only Freddy Fox who had ridden his first classic winner nearly ten years previously! Surely no boy has ever made a better start than Elliott with two winners in succession. He later won the Gold Vase and the Gold Cup at Ascot on Golden Myth, as well as the Eclipse Stakes at Sandown. Archie Falcon and I became good friends after that incident. He was a very big punter and did many commissions for me. We both had a good win when Golden Myth won at the next Newmarket meeting.

The year Golden Myth won the Gold Cup (1922), I had two other good stayers, Devizes and The Winter King. I galloped them together before Ascot and a blanket could have covered the three at the finish. I wrote straight away to Lord Rosebery advising him that The Winter King had gone so well that I thought he would win the Churchill Stakes. I was very keen for him to win as Lord Rosebery had not had an Ascot winner for several seasons. That night I found The Winter King, a son of the Derby and Oaks heroine Signorinetta, hopping lame with a splint. I could not get him out of the box for two days, but by working on his leg continuously we gradually got the soreness out. He went to Ascot without doing a canter and won his race. Devizes, with 9st. 7 on his back, was beaten a neck in the Ascot Stakes, but Golden Myth won the Gold Vase and the Gold Cup in record times.

Altogether Golden Myth won seven races and £15,266 in stakes, but good horse that he was he came near to ruining my stable as a sire. Sir George Bullough had not got a stud at the time and so we arranged for Golden Myth to stand at Lord Rosebery's stud at Mentmore. He had made such a reputation for himself on the racecourse that everyone wanted to patronise him and Sir George Bullough himself bought some mares specially to be put to him. Lord Rosebery and Sir William Cooke also sent mares to him with the result that for four years I had a stable full of Golden Myth's stock. He proved to be one of the most deplorable failures at the stud of any good horse I have known and hardly sired a winner of any description. Apart from the painful fact that most of them just could not 'go', they declined to do the little of which they were capable.

The best animal Sir George Bullough ever owned was a lovely little Blandford filly called Campanula. She won the One Thousand Guineas in 1934 after giving us a horrible fright by refusing to line up at the start. I think she was one of the most perfectly made small fillies I have ever seen. Sir George owned two other pretty good performers in Daytona and Eastern Monarch. Daytona, by Fairway, won the Select Stakes. Eastern Monarch, a grand looking horse by Lemberg, was offered for sale as a yearling by Sir

Charles Pulley, but having a curb on his hock failed to reach his reserve. I told Sir George I liked the colt and did not think the curb would ever bother him, so Sir George instructed me to take him at the reserve price. I went up to the Sale Paddocks early next morning and met the stud groom taking Eastern Monarch out of the yard en route for the station. I told him I was prepared to pay the reserve price so he took him to Park Lodge instead. He proved a pretty good but rather unlucky horse. The best race he won was the Prince of Wales's Stakes at Royal Ascot.

CHAPTER V

One day at Hurst Park I had won a race and was leaving the unsaddling enclosure when Lord Dalmeny called me aside and said he wanted to have a word with me. He first asked me whether I had been invited to take the horses of a well-known owner who was rumoured to be changing his trainer. I told Lord Dalmeny I had received no such invitation and he advised me to turn it down if it came, as his father Lord Rosebery, a former Prime Minister and a leading figure on the Turf who had owned three winners of the Derby, was going to ask me to take his horses and there would not be room at Park Lodge for Lord Rosebery's and those of the other owner as well. This was the beginning of an association which lasted forty years, a period during which I have always felt it a great honour and privilege to train the horses carrying the famous primrose and rose hoops. For most of these forty years I have been training for the present Earl of Rosebery and no one could wish for a better owner to serve. Winning or losing, he has always been the same. To have complete confidence that whatever one does will be accepted as having been done for the best is a tremendous help to a trainer and removes much of the worry from what can be a very worrying profession. If more owners adopted the same attitude as Lord Rosebery, I feel sure they would obtain better results from their horses.

Shortly after this conversation at Hurst Park, it was arranged for me to take over all old Lord Rosebery's horses from Frank Hartigan, who trained at Weyhill. Not surprisingly, Hartigan was extremely displeased and in fact he took this reversal of fortune rather badly. When my men went to Weyhill to collect the horses they were not allowed in the yard at all, the horses being led out and handed over outside. There were eighteen of them altogether—every single one was to win a race—and they were conveyed to New-market by special train.

The first morning I had them out I exercised them round a small circular canter on New Grounds and stood in the middle and watched them with my Head Man, Percy Double. We both agreed that the pick was a bay colt with a beautiful action called Ellangowan, by the Derby winner Lemberg out of Lammermuir, whose dam was one of the most famous Mentmore mares, Montem. What particularly impressed me about Ellangowan was that he moved just like his grandsire, my father's great horse Cyllene. As a two-year-old Ellangowan was backward and I felt sure he needed plenty of time. Old Lord Rosebery, unlike his son, was inclined to be impatient and somewhat difficult. He wanted Ellangowan to run but I was against it so the colt developed a cough that lasted quite a long time! We eventually brought him out at Kempton and he ran a really good race against the Duke of Westminster's Twelve Pointer, a two-year-old with top class form. I then reckoned he had done enough for his first season so he had a recurrence of his cough.

The following season I brought him out in the Craven Stakes at Newmarket. He ran second to a nice colt of Alec Taylor's and as it was only Ellangowan's second outing in public and his first one of the season, he pleased me very much indeed. His next race was the Two Thousand Guineas and in a desperate finish, beautifully ridden by Elliott, he won by a head from Lord Woolavington's Knockando. He did not really stay more than ten furlongs and in the Derby he ran well for that distance, the race being won by Papyrus, trained by my brother Basil. Ellangowan won the St. James's Palace Stakes at Ascot and the Champion Stakes later that season. In his only race as a four-year-old he carried 9st. 12 in the Prince of Wales's Stakes at Kempton and was beaten by Hobgoblin to whom he was conceding 26lbs.

At the close of Ellangowan's career as a four-year-old Lord Rosebery decided to sell him together with a three-year-old called Parmenio that had run fourth to Sansovino in the 1924 Derby. At this time Lord Rosebery owned a little three-year-old called Poetaster, who had won a race but had been rather unlucky and been beaten several times when I fancied him. On one occasion I had written to Lord Rosebery saying I proposed to run Poetaster somewhere, to which Lord Rosebery wrote back saying he could not think why I kept running him 'as he never wins'. I therefore did not run him on that occasion, but later, thinking Lord Rosebery would have forgotten by then, I ran him at Derby. Once again he was unlucky as he got kicked at the post and was beaten. I was the recipient of a sarcastic letter the very next day.

Shortly before the December Sales I wrote to Lord Rosebery saying that I had entered Ellangowan, Parmenio and Poetaster for the December Sales as instructed and would like to know what reserves should be placed on them. I was told to consult Lord Dalmeny and Mr. Edmunds, the Mentmore Stud Manager, on that point. I suggested higher figures for Ellangowan and Parmenio than did Lord Dalmeny and Mr. Edmunds, but was informed that if Lord Rosebery put horses into a sale he wanted to sell them and would be extremely put out if they failed to reach their reserve. Eventually we compromised on a valuation and I wrote to inform Lord Rosebery, adding that Poetaster would go up without reserve.

To our horror neither Ellangowan nor Parmenio reached their reserve and Poetaster only made about 700 guineas. After this fiasco Lord Dalmeny and Mr. Edmunds came to my house and told me that it was my job to write and tell Lord Rosebery, adding for my comfort that he was sure to be furious. I waited with a certain anxiety for the reply which came as follows:

'Jarvis,
        I condole with you on the loss of Poetaster, whom you were so fond of seeing run.
                                                    R.'

Lord Rosebery always wrote on black-edged paper after the death of his second son, the Hon. Neil Primrose, who was killed in the war. His letters to me invariably started 'Jarvis' and he never signed them more fully than 'R'. I once ran a horse of his, which was unplaced, on the first day of the season at Lincoln. The next day I received a letter which ran as follows:

'Jarvis,
      I fear we have got into a vein of also-rans.

R.'

I eventually wrote to Lord Rosebery offering the reserve price for Ellangowan, which was accepted. Sir John Fox and Mr. Rowland Rank came in with me and although he was not a great success as a sire, we got our money back several times over. One of the best horses Ellangowan got was Tartan, a half-brother to Blue Peter. Although a mile was probably Tartan's best distance, he became in due course a famous sire of jumpers, among his progeny being the Grand National winner Royal Tan and that magnificent chaser Saffron Tartan, winner of the Gold Cup at Cheltenham. Among the races Tartan himself won was the Britannia Stakes at Ascot. This was a race that in fact had been included in the Royal Ascot programme on my suggestion as there was no mile handicap confined to three-year-olds at the meeting. I made the suggestion to the present Lord Rosebery, who forwarded it to the Ascot Authority.

A very good filly I trained for Lord Rosebery was Plack by Hurry On out of Groat, a grandaughter of Montem. A great big chestnut filly with enormous feet and ears, she was extremely temperamental but in a race as game as could be. She always showed signs of making a stayer and as a two-year-old she won the Lennox Plate at Hurst Park, the Rous Plate at Doncaster and a mile nursery at Ayr. She wintered exceptionally well and I began to think she would have a chance in the classics even though she would come up against the Aga Khan's brilliant grey filly Mumtaz Mahal. When the One Thousand Guineas came along, there was not only Mumtaz Mahal to beat, but another great filly in Sir Edward Hulton's Straitlace, by Son-In-Law, and things did not look at all easy when Plack came dead in season on the day of the race and cantered down to the post swishing her tail in ominous fashion. Despite doubts about her stamina, Mumtaz Mahal started a hot favourite at 6/5. Straitlace was a well-backed second favourite at 7/2, while there was plenty of support for Plack at 8/1.

Mumtaz Mahal set off at a terrific pace and at the Bushes she must have been six lengths ahead of the next group which was headed by Straitlace and Plack. At that point it really looked as if 'The Flying Filly' would never be caught. She came down the hill easily enough with Hulme showing no sign of anxiety, but as soon as she met the rising ground her stride began to shorten. Straitlace closed the gap and it seemed certain that the stamina she had shown the previous season would enable her to win, but suddenly she faltered and her chance had gone. In the meantime Charlie Elliott on Plack had been making ground up steadily and coming into the Dip my filly was barely a length behind the leader. On the hill she collared Mumtaz, who was changing her legs and had become slightly unbalanced, and with her tail revolving like a windmill she ran on to win by a length and a half,

47

with Straitlace half a length away third. It cannot be often that fillies as good as these have occupied the first three places in the One Thousand. All three have, through their descendants, made their mark in the Stud Book, too.

In the Oaks Straitlace reversed the positions. Plack was ideally placed at Tattenham Corner, but then for some reason she lost her place. She was running on strongly again at the finish and ended up third. I always thought she was a bit unlucky not to win. We kept her in training in the hope that she would win an Ascot Gold Cup, a race Lord Rosebery had never won. She might well have pulled it off, but when travelling really well she was badly struck into by Papyrus and her chance was ruined. Because of this, Lord Rosebery always refused to send any mare of his to Papyrus. Altogether Plack won 9 races worth £11,467, her victories, besides the One Thousand Guineas, including the Newmarket Oaks and the Jockey Club Cup.

Like Lord Rosebery, Plack had whims of her own to which attention had to be given. For example she would never consent to walk under the railway bridge near my place unless we sent a man down to lead her. He only had to rest a hand on the rein and she would walk quietly under the bridge; if that routine was omitted, she would whip round and play merry hell. For five years running after 1933 Plack did not produce a foal. She was then, at the age of seventeen, mated with the not particularly distinguished stallion Obliterate, who was the same age as herself. She duly produced a filly appropriately named After-thought, who emulated her mother by winning the

48

Lord Rosebery's Miracle, bought for 170 guineas as a yearling and winner of the Gimcrack Stakes, Newmarket Stakes and Eclipse Stakes.

Lord Rosebery's Sandwich, Harry Wragg up—winner of the
St Leger and very unlucky not to win the Derby.

Jockey Club Cup, besides being placed in the Oaks, the Gold Cup and the Champion Stakes. Plack died in 1940.

Another good staying filly I trained for the old Earl was Bongrace, foaled in 1923, by Spion Kop out of Vaucluse. Full of courage, she needed a tremendous amount of work at home and was liable to become 'set fast' if she was given an easy day. Altogether she won eight races, including the Doncaster and Jockey Club Cups and the Newmarket Oaks.

Bongrace was certainly one of the laziest fillies I have ever trained and she would do nothing without a smack with the whip. On two occasions her jockey dropped his whip and each time it cost her the race. She was ridden in the Oaks by Charlie Elliott. At the top of the hill she was well placed, but suddenly began to drop back. Elliott went for his whip to give her a reminder, but it was knocked flying out of his hand. She kept losing ground till our other runner, ridden by Henri Jelliss was passing her. Elliott shouted to Jelliss to give him his whip, but between them they managed to drop it. Eventually Elliott was handed a whip by Steve Donoghue when the pair of them were somewhere near the tail end of the field. Elliott gave Bongrace a reminder and she fairly flew, only just missing a place in the end.

In the autumn of the same year Bongrace ran in the Doncaster Cup ridden by Fred Fox. She and Glommen, a good stayer of Mr. S. B. Joel's were fighting it out when Glommen rolled on to her and knocked the whip out of Fox's hand. Glommen was first past the post but we objected and got the race. We were sharply criticised for objecting, but I think

49

we were right. In the Jockey Club Cup at Newmarket the following month, Glommen and Bongrace were both engaged again. I told Lord Dalmeny I intended to run Bongrace although she met Glommen on 12lbs. worse terms, just to show how right we had been to object at Doncaster. In a great finish Bongrace beat Glommen, who had won the Goodwood Cup that summer, and an even better stayer in Foxlaw, who won the Gold Cup the following year. The next season Bongrace must have put her foot in a hole when running for the Kempton Jubilee, as she broke down badly on her off hind and could never run again. Among her winners at the stud was Ribbon, a filly by Fairway which she produced at the age of seventeen. Ribbon inherited all her mother's gameness. As a two-year-old she won the Middle Park Stakes, beating Nasrullah by a head. The following season she was beaten a neck in the One Thousand Guineas by Herringbone, a neck by Why Hurry in the Oaks, and a short head by Herringbone in the St. Leger.

Lord Rosebery had a colt by Spion Kop out of Valescure which he named The Bastard. I was having lunch with Lord Rosebery one day at The Durdans, his house at Epsom, when he remarked, 'I hear I have been criticised for the naming of The Bastard.' I replied that I had heard a few comments about it. 'Well, they have not read their Shakespeare,' he said. Although not more than a very useful colt The Bastard became quite famous. He ran in a race at Newmarket on the July Course on July 2nd, 1929, the very first day that the tote ever operated in this country. The bookmakers had rather lost their heads and were endeavouring to beat the tote by laying extended odds so that when The Bastard won he was returned at 100/1. It was my first year as a member of the Twelve Club, the members of which nominate twelve horses at the beginning of the season and score points according to the odds at which those horses win. I had nominated The Bastard among my dozen and his win knocked the bottom out of the competition that year which I won with ease. I now have the honour of being President of the Twelve Club, which is limited to a hundred members, all good sportsmen.

The Bastard was eventually sold to go to Australia where the Aussies were so shocked at his name that they altered it to The Buzzard lest anyone's suscepti-bilities should be injured. He did extremely well at the stud, living to a great age and heading the sires' list on more than one occasion. A year or two ago I was in Sydney when a journalist came to interview me. He said he was not a racing man, but asked me to give him a story. I told him I had trained The Bastard in England and that I had been very amused at the change of name as the Aussies I had met in the 1914 war had used the word almost as a term of endear-ment. The next day the whole story was in one of the leading newspapers underneath a photograph of my-self and the heading 'He Has Been Laughing At Us For 20 Years'.

Midlothian, a half-brother to Ellangowan by that great stayer Son-In-Law, was a pretty good three-year-old and in one of the most tremendous finishes I have ever seen, he was beaten a couple of heads in the 1929 Newmarket Stakes by Lord Derby's Hunters

Moon and Major D. McCalmont's Guineas winner Mr. Jinks. As a result of his running in that race Midlothian was backed for the Derby, but just before Epsom Lord Rosebery died and Midlothian's entry for the Derby became void according to the rule that was then in force. Fortunately this rule, as a result of a friendly action between Mr. Edgar Wallace and the Jockey Club, was altered in time for Cameronian to win the Derby two years later.

Old Lord Rosebery was invariably courteous but he could be formidable, too, and was the last man in the world with whom it was advisable to take a liberty. His comments sometimes carried a sting at the tail and he possessed the ability to deflate you in two or three words. I recollect that on one occasion he introduced me to his grandson Ronald Primrose, a fine athlete and a great sportsman who was destined to die tragically young when up at Oxford. 'I want you to meet Mr. Jarvis,' said Lord Rosebery, 'who has trained a great many winners for me.' He then added as an afterthought, 'But not recently.' In his racing ventures Lord Rosebery could be easily discouraged. I remember one year I took several of his horses up to Ayr where I shared a house with Frank Barling and Walter Earl. On the first two days Lord Rosebery's horses were unsuccessful and I received a telegram from him on the second evening ordering me to send all his horses back to Newmarket forthwith. Now Bongrace was running on the third day and I fancied her a lot so I wired to Lord Rosebery saying I expected her to win and requesting permission to run her. I received a very frosty negative by return.

When Lord Rosebery was dying, I went to Epsom to see Lord Dalmeny at The Durdans. I remember we were talking together in the grounds when he told me that his father was unlikely to live through the night. Lord Rosebery died the next day. A brilliant man who had been a great supporter of the Turf, he was succeeded by one who was destined to play an even greater part in the racing world as owner, breeder and administrator.

CHAPTER VI

I have been extraordinarily lucky with the first horses I have bought for many of my owners. For one of my earliest patrons, Mr. Arthur Gunn, I bought Fiddlededee, a fine sprinter who was always running gallantly under big weights and whose successes included the Molyneux Cup at Liverpool. Golden Myth, about whom I have already written, was the first horse I bought for Sir George Bullough. Sir George was a tall, thin Scot who, when he was at Newmarket hated to miss his afternoon round of golf and usually played with William Halsey, the former jockey. If Halsey was not available, Sir George trudged round on his own, with a caddy in attendance. The weather had to be unspeakable to stop him from playing. One afternoon four of us were going to play a foursome but the rain teemed down and Dick Perryman decided it was too wet and stayed at home. The rest of us sat in the club-house—formerly the grandstand on the long defunct steeplechase course— and waited for the rain to stop. Suddenly we saw Sir George emerge, and accompanied by a somewhat reluctant caddy, head for the first tee. As Sir George was considerably older than any of us, our consciences were slightly pricked and we decided we must face the elements, too. I accordingly asked Sir George if he would care to take Perryman's place and join us. When I explained that Perryman had thought it too wet, Sir George was obviously surprised. 'Too wet?' he said 'It's perfectly all right. You can see the ball!'

I had a long and very happy association with Lord Milford, who was Sir Laurence Philipps when he first became a patron of Park Lodge. This tall, courteous Welshman was the sixth son of Canon Sir James Philipps, 12th Baronet, and two of his older brothers were also created peers. He himself founded the Court Line, of which he himself acted as chairman. Among other business activities he was largely instrumental in founding Tote Investors Ltd., the famous credit service of the Tote.

I first met Lord Milford through my interest in coursing, a great sport in my opinion and one to which I have always been addicted. It was a very big moment in my life when I won the 'Blue Riband' of coursing, the Waterloo Cup, with Jovial Judge. One day the late Lord Sefton, another coursing enthusiast, suggested to me that I should restart coursing at Newmarket and try and revive the Champion Puppy Stakes. This seemed a good idea to me and I went into action supported by Mr. Sydney Beer, who agreed to put up a cup, Monty Collis-Browne, Colonel McCalmont and the Reverend Brocklebank. On hearing what was afoot, Mr. Stollery, proprietor of the famous Barbican greyhound repository, asked if we could handle a 64 dog stake as he would like to stage the Barbican Cup there, having fallen out with some farmers at Peterborough where it had been previously run.

Forthwith I set off to see three landowners who all had big shoots in the locality, Lord Milford of Six Mile Bottom, Captain King of Hare Park and Lord Ellesmere of Stetchworth. They all agreed to let me have the meeting on their shooting land. As it happened, there was a severe frost and the meeting had to be postponed. Lord Ellesmere and Captain King had no objection to the postponement, but Lord Milford objected on the grounds that it would be too late in the year and would interfere with the shooting. It was unfortunate to say the least that at this somewhat tricky juncture our secretary, Monty Collis-Browne, was on tour with the Cambridge University football team, of which he was a devoted supporter, and letters sent to apprise him of our trouble never succeeded in catching up with him. In the end I went to see Lord Milford myself and persuaded him that his shooting would not be impeded or harmed in any way. As a matter of fact I won the Barbican Cup myself with Junior Journalist, a litter brother of Jovial Judge, and as he was a mere puppy taking on older dogs I managed to secure a nice bet of £1,000 to 6.

The following July, Lord Milford rang me up and said: 'My wife takes me racing and I get terribly bored. If I had a horse or two I might find it more interesting.' The upshot was that he asked me to spend £10,000 on three yearlings for him.

The very first yearling I purchased on his behalf was Flamingo, a bay colt by Flamboyant, winner of the Goodwood and Doncaster Cups, out of Lady Peregrine, by that fine sire of brood mares, White Eagle. A beautifully made little colt, Flamingo, foaled in 1925 at Sir John Robinson's Worksop Manor Stud, proved a top class two-year-old, winning the Spring Stakes and Fulbourne Stakes at Newmarket and also the National Breeders' Produce Stakes at Sandown, then the most valuable two-year-old event of the season. This was a striking example of beginner's luck, but there was better still to come. The following spring Flamingo won the Column Produce Stakes at the Craven Meeting and then the Two Thousand Guineas in which he had a terrific battle with Royal Minstrel, a big, handsome grey by Tetratema that Cecil Boyd-Rochfort trained for Captain G. P. Gough. Royal Minstrel, who later won the St. James's Palace Stakes, Eclipse Stakes and Victoria Cup, did not come down the hill quite as smoothly as Flamingo who battled on with his usual gameness to win by inches.

To my dying day I shall always be convinced that Flamingo ought to have won the Derby instead of finishing second to Sir Hugo Cunliffe-Owen's Felstead. As in the Two Thousand Guineas, Charlie Elliott was up on Flamingo while Gordon Richards rode another fancied colt called Sunny Trace. Now at this particular epoch there was a craze for forcing the pace in the Derby. Call Boy and Coronach had both won after making virtually all the running, while Sansovino and Manna both had the race at their mercy by the time Tattenham Corner was reached. Be that as it may, Elliott and Richards set off from the start as if they were racing over five furlongs and not a mile and a half. You can imagine what my feelings were as with whips up they raced neck and neck round Tattenham Corner at a pace they could obviously not hope to maintain. With three furlongs to go they were still in front but I noticed that Felstead had improved his position and was travelling ominously well.

A quarter of a mile from home Sunny Trace was beat to the wide and dropped right out of the struggle. Flamingo continued to battle on with wonderful courage but Felstead, ridden with perfect judgment by Harry Wragg, was too strong for him in the final furlong and won by a length and a half. I think it was a wonderful performance on Flamingo's part and my own impression of the race is confirmed by the description of it given in the Bloodstock Breeders Review for that year. Looking back on it, it is only fair to say that Lord Derby's Fairway was probably the pick of the three-year-olds in 1928. He was a highly-strung individual, though, and unfortunately for his owner, Lord Derby, and for his backers, the crowd got out of control before the Derby and literally mobbed him, pulling hairs out of his tail by the handful. Not surprisingly he was a beaten horse before he had reached the starting gate. However, he won the Eclipse Stakes and also the St. Leger, in which Flamingo finished fourth. The Gold Cup was to be Flamingo's objective as a four-year-old but unfortunately he did not stand training.

As it happened Flamingo was Lord Milford's only classic winner though Horus, a half-brother to Flamingo by Papyrus was third in the St. Leger; Challenge was second in the St. Leger; Sybil's Nephew second in the Derby; and Alpine Bloom third in the One Thousand Guineas.

Flamingo was not an outstanding success as a sire

58

but he did get one notable winner for Lord Milford in Flyon, who, ridden by Eph Smith, won the 1939 Gold Cup at 100/6. When Sir John Robinson died in 1929 his bloodstock were dispersed at the December Sales. Lord Milford bought Flamingo's dam Lady Peregrine for 9,200 guineas. She proved well worth the money and among her winners was Honey Buzzard, by Papyrus, the dam of that great sprinter Honeyway. I shall have more to say about Honeyway when we come to the post-war era. Lord Milford was eighty when he died in 1962. In his last years he handed over nearly all his stud and his racing interests to his son, Mr. Jim Philipps. From the moment Flamingo won his first race, racing no longer bored Lord Milford; very much the reverse in fact, and he once told me he made a point at home of having a form-book placed beside every chair he used to sit in.

A good horse by Flamingo was Lord Rosebery's Flamenco, a half-brother to The Bastard whom I have previously mentioned. Flamenco, who turned out to be a highly successful sire of jumpers, won the Lincoln as a four-year-old with 9 stone. I felt pretty confident and he started at 8/1. We had a very nice win. It was Eph Smith's first big win for me.

Flamenco's most famous victory, though, was in the St. James's Palace Stakes at Royal Ascot the previous year. In that race he defeated Lord Glanely's Colombo, winner of the Two Thousand Guineas and third to Windsor Lad and Easton in the Derby. A lot of people had blamed his rider, Ray Johnstone, for that Epsom defeat, but in my view that was unfair; Colombo just did not stay.

In those days I used to take a house for Ascot week

at Kennell Ride, one of the attractions besides its proximity to the course being that it had eight boxes attached. My friend Captain 'Sam' Long, for many years 'Augur' of the *Sporting Life*, stayed in a nearby house with a number of jockeys. On the Tuesday morning Sam and I were out early on the racecourse. We wanted to see the French Gold Cup horse, Thor II, work but as it happened he was later than we anticipated in making his appearance so we strolled together round the course. It was then that I noticed that whereas the ground on the inside near the rails had been well watered so that the grass was lush and strong, the ground on the far side of the course showed little evidence of watering and was firm and fast. Clearly any horses running on the wide outside would secure a decisive advantage and I made my plan accordingly.

There were only four runners for the St. James's Palace Stakes which was then, as now, the last event on the card of the opening day. The race is run over the Old Mile and I told Flamenco's rider Harry Wragg to keep on the left hand side of the track on the firm going. The advantage he gained proved well worth the ground he inevitably lost crossing to the outside before the turn. Colombo could never quite get to him and Flamenco held on to win a truly sensational race by half a length. It was a real old-fashioned Ascot turn-up and the tactics adopted on Flamenco were the talk of the meeting. We tried the same dodge on Honey Buzzard, a 20/1 outsider, in the Coronation Stakes, also run over the Old Mile. She only failed by a neck to beat Foxcroft, trained by Boyd-Rochfort, and finished a long way in front of the Oaks winner Light Brocade. Unfortunately Joe Childs, who rode Foxcroft, had picked up the tip from seeing Flamenco win and pursued the same tactics as we did. I almost brought it off again in the St. James's Palace Stakes in 1955 when conditions were almost the same. Tamerlane, 11/8 on, just caught my 20/1 outsider, Blue Blazes, and beat him a head.

I first met Sir Allan Gordon-Smith, founder of the clock-making and motor-car accessory business, S. Smith and Sons, through a common love of coursing, Sir Allan having won the Waterloo Cup with Golden Seal in 1927 and with Golden Surprise two years later. In 1936 he asked me to buy him a yearling, preferably a stayer. First of all I chose for him a very attractive yearling bred by Colonel Loder and it was decided that if the price was right, that would be the one I should buy. A bit later, though, I took a great fancy to a colt by the Gold Cup winner Foxlaw out of Molly Adare, a Phalaris mare whose grandam was the immortal Pretty Polly. As the Foxlaw colt was clearly bred to stay while the other one I had chosen was not, I eventually bought the former, for the eminently reasonable price of 620 guineas.

Once again it was a case of the first horse I bought for an owner proving lucky although in this case the luck took plenty of time to materialise, as like most of the Son-In-Law tribe, he took a long time to come to hand. In fact at the end of his second season, Fearless Fox, as he had been named, was still a maiden. He had run some very good races, though, as he had been second in the Newmarket Stakes, the Gold Vase and the St. Leger. Fortunately Sir Allan was a very patient man and I told him that I would undertake to win the Ascot Gold Vase for him in 1937. Fearless Fox duly obliged in that event and as he had not been subjected to an exacting race I decided to run him in the Gold Cup two days later. In a field of twelve he was soundly backed at 6/1 but finished unplaced behind that very good horse Precipitation.

It gives me little pleasure to recall the unfortunate repercussions of that race. It had seemed to me that Fearless Fox got a very rough passage and I was genuinely under the impression that a certain jockey was less concerned with winning the race than with roughing up Fearless Fox, who had paint from the rails on his flank when he returned to the paddock. In those days trainers were allowed in the jockeys' changing room and I was talking about the race to Eph Smith when Bill Rickaby came up and corroborated what Smith had told me, saying that he had pulled out from behind Fearless Fox as he thought Fearless Fox was going to be brought down.

Now I have never been accused of being a vindictive man but I admit to possessing a temper, the combustion point of which is fairly low. Of course I was quite wrong to do it and I regret still the words that I used, but I could not restrain myself from tearing a considerable strip off the jockey I deemed to have offended. I certainly should not have used the expression 'Irish Bastard', particularly as the jockey in question was born in Scotland. I was just beginning to cool off and dismiss the whole incident from my mind when I was sent for by the Stewards. I thought they were inquiring into incidents during the race, but to my surprise and annoyance I was in fact 'on the mat' for my remarks to the jockey and was

duly fined £25 by Lord Hamilton. Of course nowadays the situation would be very different as the
patrol camera could provide incontrovertible evidence.

Nor did this sorry business end with my fine. I was
sued for slander by the aggrieved jockey, who was
represented by the formidable Sir Patrick Hastings,
KC., while Sir Norman Birkett KC. (later Lord
Birkett) appeared for me. Eventually the case was
settled out of court. I have exchanged words with the
jockey concerned since then, but the likelihood of
our ever becoming friends can be regarded as slender.

It was some consolation that Fearless Fox won the
Goodwood Cup, beating a strong field that included
the Gold Cup winner Quashed, one of the gamest
mares I have ever seen, Cecil and Enfield. That night
Sir Allan gave a big celebration party and presented
me with a gold cigarette box as a token of Fearless
Fox's Gold Vase success. Inside the lid were a few
lines of verse which commemorated in light-hearted
fashion my misfortunes at Ascot. Sir Allan having
won the big race that afternoon at what was his home
meeting, it was some party, I can assure you! Fearless
Fox was a very game horse and ran a great race in the
Doncaster Cup, being beaten a head by Haulfryn, a
horse of the same age to whom he was conceding
10lbs.

I always thought Sir Allan was unlucky not to win
the Grand National. In 1947 he was third with Kami,
ridden by John Hislop. Not long afterwards his fine
chaser Cloncarrig was much fancied to win but parted
company with John Hislop just before halfway. In
1950, ridden this time by Bob Turnell, Cloncarrig

was level with the eventual winner, Freebooter, and going every bit as well when he came down two fences from home. When Gordon, as I always called him, died I lost one of my greatest and best-loved friends.

The first horse I bought for Lord Wimborne, who did not, however, remain in racing for very long, was Fancy Free who won four races and in due course became the dam of the Derby winner Blue Peter, by far the best horse I have ever trained.

For Sir John Jarvis the first horse I bought was Golden Martlet who won first time out. He proved quite useful and won several races, but Sir John subsequently owned a good many better than him, including Royal Charger who was third in the Two Thousand Guineas and in 1946 won the Ayr Gold Cup as a four-year-old with 9st. 7. A big handsome horse by Nearco, he was sold at the end of his racing career, to the Irish National Stud for 50,000 guineas. In 1953 he was re-sold to go to America where he proved a great success as a sire. Another good horse I bought for Sir John Jarvis was Old Reliance, a very fast gelding by an unfashionable sire called Old Rowley, a son of The Tetrarch.

Originally bought for 150 guineas as a yearling, Old Reliance was first owned and trained by Herbert Blagrave, for whom he ran a good second with a stiff weight in the 1938 Stewards Cup at Goodwood. I then bought him for Sir John for whom he proceeded to win the Ayr Gold Cup under 9st. 2, a big weight for a three-year-old. The following summer Old Reliance won the Cork and Orrery Stakes at Royal Ascot. Because he was a gelding we let him go to India in 1940. I had also won the Ayr Gold Cup in 1937, on that

64

Blue Peter—the best horse I ever trained.

Blue Peter (No. 5) winning the Eclipse Stakes.

occasion with Sir George Bullough's Daytona. After Old Reliance's victory, the Cup was not competed for again until 1946, the year I won with Royal Charger. Thus I had won the Cup three times in succession, but there was a gap of eight years between the second victory and the third. Ayr is undoubtedly Scotland's premier course and since Lord Rosebery likes to see his colours carried there, I have always been a strong supporter of the September meeting and my successes there now number a hundred. I was very touched and honoured in 1965 when Lord Howard de Walden, on behalf of the Ayr executive, presented me with a very nice cigar box. It was exactly sixty years after I had ridden Kilglass to victory in the Ayr Gold Cup for Lord Howard de Walden's father.

Other good horses I trained for Sir John Jarvis were Gainsborough Lass who was a sister of the Two Thousand Guineas winner Orwell and won the Coronation Stakes at Ascot; Veuve Clicquot, twice winner of the King George Stakes at Goodwood; Faerie Queen, winner of the Scottish Derby and the Newmarket Oaks; Admiral's Walk, second to Blue Peter in the Two Thousand Guineas and winner of the St. James's Palace Stakes; and Reynard Volant, winner of the Ascot Stakes two years running.

I first met Sir John Jarvis in rather a curious way. Owing to a clerical error, my account from Ladbrokes was received by Sir John who forwarded it on to me with a facetious note and the hope that one day we should meet. Not long afterwards, while staying with Monty Collis-Browne for Goodwood, we motored past Sir John's place, Hascombe Court, near

Godalming. Monty told me who lived there and I suggested that we should go in and call as Sir John had expressed the wish to meet me. My first impression was that Sir John was not noticeably pleased at receiving visitors but when I explained my identity he became very friendly and not long afterwards he asked me to buy some yearlings for him. Actually before I bought any yearlings for him he wanted me to bid on his behalf for Solario, who was coming up for sale as a stallion. That transaction, though, did not materialise.

After Sir John's death in 1950 I trained for his son, Sir Adrian Jarvis, until the latter's sad and very sudden death in 1965. Sir Adrian's best horses were Tessa Gillian who was second to my other runner, Happy Laughter, in the 1953 One Thousand Guineas; and Test Case, winner of the Gimcrack Stakes in 1960.

An owner for whom I trained a lot of winners between the wars was Mr. Edward Esmond. He was in fact an outstanding personality in international racing and his colours were frequently successful, not only in England and France, but also in India where he raced in association with his brother, Sir Edward Ezra. The best horse of many top class performers Frank Carter trained for him in France was Hotweed, winner of the Grand Prix, the French Derby and the French Gold Cup. Unfortunately Hotweed's temperament was the reverse of docile and he failed as a sire. It was Mr. Esmond who purchased the great Italian horse Donatello II who, so I am told, was desperately unlucky to be beaten in the Grand Prix. Donatello II sired two great horses in Crepello and

66

Alycidon as well as the dams of Pinza and Aureole.

Mr. Esmond's name first became familiar with English racegoers when he paid 17,000 guineas for the Oaks winner Straitlace at the Hulton dispersal in 1925. He was introduced to me by Lord Rosebery and became a patron of my stable in 1926. The first horse I bought for Mr. Esmond was Foxhunter, who was bred by Lord St. Davids and was a half-brother to the dual Gold Cup winner Trimdon by the Gold Cup winner Foxlaw. Not a bad pedigree for a stayer! Like most of his breed Foxhunter was slow to develop but he was a very useful three-year-old, winning the Tudor Stakes at Sandown and the Doncaster Cup. He continued to improve and on his first appearance as a four-year-old he won the Queen's Prize at Kempton with 9st. 2. His target at Ascot was of course the Gold Cup, but I had a notion that a run in the Churchill Stakes over two miles the day before would just about bring him to his best, particularly as he appeared in that event to have a comparatively easy task. Starting at 5/4 on, he was beaten a neck by Beau Frère, a colt of his own age to whom he was conceding 28lbs., the pair finishing lengths ahead of the remainder.

The consequence of that race was that most people dismissed Foxhunter from their Gold Cup calculations and he started at 25/1. To their surprise if not entirely to mine, he won by a length defeating a strong field that included Orpen second in the Derby and the St. Leger; Firdaussi, winner of the St. Leger; and Brulette, winner of the Oaks. In the Goodwood Cup Foxhunter started at 11/4 on but broke down and never ran again. It should have afforded Mr. Esmond a certain satisfaction that the Cup was won by his three-year-old Sans Peine, acting as pacemaker for Foxhunter, but he failed to recognise his second colours on Sans Peine and was quite unaware that a horse of his had won. Foxhunter might have been a great sire if the luck had gone his way. He started his stud career in France and was just establishing himself when the war came and he was transferred to England. There he remained for five years with very few chances. At the ripe age of sixteen he was exported to Argentina where he proved an immense success.

Poor Mr. Esmond was in Scotland when war broke out and he remained there until April when, rashly as things turned out, he returned to Paris. When France was overrun he escaped with difficulty and it was only after considerable hardships that he eventually reached America. He longed to return to Europe and being a great lover of the thoroughbred, it broke his heart when he heard that the Nazis, venting their vindictive spite against a non-aryan owner, had broken up his stable and dispersed his horses. He felt that he was too old and too tired to contemplate starting afresh. He never saw Europe again and died in New York in 1945.

Mr. Esmond was a keen golfer and by most diligent practice had made himself into a pretty good one; good enough at any rate to win the famous Worplesdon Mixed Foursomes with the great Joyce Wethered (Lady Heathcote-Amory) as his partner. His daughters were excellent golfers, too. When I was up in Scotland in the autumn I always used to go to North Berwick to stay with Mr. Esmond and invariably I played a game of golf in which two of the three other players were those giants of the game, Roger Wethered and Cyril Tolley, both previous amateur champions. I felt I was running a bit out of my class in that company but the result of the match did not matter; the important thing was for me to tip a winner to the caddies.

Two other patrons of my stable were Mr. Charles Gordon and Sir Lewis Richardson. Mr. Charles Gordon was a man of outstanding charm and I enjoyed a very long and extremely happy association with him. He did pretty well with horses he bred himself, among which were Sea Bequest, third to Bahram in the 1935 Two Thousand Guineas, and Fair Judgement who landed a gamble in the 1949 Lincoln. In his prime Mr. Gordon was a fine player of real tennis and was once runner-up to the great Edgar Baerlein, father of the racing correspondent Richard Baerlein, in the amateur championship. I am delighted to say that one of Mr. Gordon's charming daughters, Mrs. Michael Gordon-Watson, now has a horse in my stable.

Sir Lewis Richardson was a South African and the very first horse I bought for him was Heverswood, who in 1924 won the Portland Handicap with 8st. 12, a record weight for a three-year-old in that event till Mr. Sydney Beer's Diomedes won the following year with 9st. 2. Mr. Beer subsequently owned a useful sprinter called Figaro. I remember one day my wife asked Mr. Beer whether Figaro was pronounced with a long a or a short one as the owners of a shop called Figaro's always pronounced it with a long a. Mr. Beer, who is a very talented musician, replied with just a hint of pretentiousness '*Mo*zart always called it Figăro'. 'Never mind Mozart,' I replied, 'the important thing is what does Mo Tarsh call it?'*

* For the uninitiated Mo Tarsh was a famous course bookmaker between the wars.

CHAPTER VII

The Blue Peter story really dates back to a day in 1925 when Lord Rosebery (he was Lord Dalmeny then) rang me up and told me that Lord Wimborne was giving up polo and wanted to start a small stud, primarily to find an occupation for his stud groom. Lord Rosebery suggested I might find something suitable at the Hulton dispersal, but buyers seemed to go mad at that particular sale and the prices realised were far above the valuations I made.

However at the Doncaster Sales that year I bought three fillies for Lord Wimborne. The first was Fancy Free who had attracted my attention by virtue of the fact that she was a beautiful walker. Her sire was Stefan the Great, a son of The Tetrarch. I did not much care for this as Stefan the Great was out of Perfect Peach, most of whose offspring possessed undoubted ability but unfortunately were very far from genuine. However I noticed that Fancy Free's dam Celiba went back to a very good mare called Palmflower, who was not only a good race-mare herself but had produced winners of over £26,000 in stakes, a lot of money in those days. Moreover I had at home one of Palmflower's hooves, beautifully fashioned into an inkstand. On account of Palmflower I over-looked my prejudice against Stefan the Great and purchased Fancy Free. I also bought for Lord Wimborne a filly by Buchan called All's Blue and a White Eagle filly that made a noise and never saw a race-course.

Fancy Free proved quite a good performer and as a three-year-old won races to the value of £2,447, including the Great Midland Breeders Plate at Nottingham and the Whitsuntide Handicap at Hurst Park. Lord Wimborne took only scant interest and never came to see her run. It was no surprise to me when he decided to chuck racing and offered his stock to Lord Rosebery for what seemed a reasonable sum. Lord Rosebery asked me whether I advised him to accept and I strongly urged him to do so. Before she produced Blue Peter, Fancy Free had bred four winners. These included Tartan, by Ellangowan, winner of the Britannia Stakes and three other races, and a great sire of jumpers; Springtime, by Apelle, who bred eleven winners and became one of the foundation mares of Major Lionel Holliday's stud; Full Sail, by Fairway, who won the National Breeders' Produce Stakes at Sandown and became a leading sire in South America ; and Flapper, by Felstead, who bred eight winners.

Foaled in 1936 at Mentmore, Blue Peter was a really beautiful chestnut colt by Fairway and thus a full brother to Full Sail. From his earliest days he showed the highest promise and on Derby Day he was a magnificent stamp of thoroughbred, standing 16.0¾ hands and with a girth of 74 inches. Below the knee he measured exactly eight inches of bone. He was less

72

highly strung than many of Fairway's stock and both in and out of the stable you could not have found a kinder horse. With his quality head and bold outlook he was difficult indeed to fault. One or two critics thought he was a bit too long behind the saddle, but so have been many other top-class horses.

Blue Peter was reared at the Sandwich Stud, Newmarket, where Lord Rosebery had another colt of high promise called Titan, and when he went into training Lord Rosebery and I agreed that we would not really bother about him as a two-year-old but would give him every chance to develop his strength and then aim at the Derby. He did not in fact run as a two-year-old until September when he finished fourth in the Imperial Produce Stakes at Kempton to Lord Derby's Heliopolis. He was still very backward and I told Eph Smith to be very careful with him. I was so greatly impressed with Blue Peter's running that I wired Lord Rosebery to that effect. Lord Rosebery later observed that I had never done such a thing before; I replied that never before had I had a horse good enough! Blue Peter ran once more that autumn, finishing second in the Middle Park Stakes to Mr. W. Woodward's very fast American-bred colt Foxbrough II.

Blue Peter thrived during the winter. The first race we gave him was the Blue Riband Trial Stakes at Epsom run over the final mile of the Derby course. He was probably the most backward member of the field but he won with impressive ease. As I watched him coming down the hill in such smooth and effortless style, I knew that bar some cruel mischance he would win the Derby. I was ill myself at the time and my doctor warned me that if I went to Epsom I did so entirely at my own risk. I was determined, though, to see the race. I left Newmarket well after mid-day and flew from the racecourse stands to Brooklands where a car awaited me to take me to Epsom. I watched the race from Sir Allan Gordon-Smith's box, and being strung up and in a somewhat emotional state, I dissolved into tears as I saw Blue Peter stride away to victory. I then flew back to Newmarket and was in bed again at 5 p.m. which was quite good going.

When Pretendre won the Blue Riband Trial Stakes twenty-seven years later, I felt about him much as I had felt about Blue Peter and I always reckon Pretendre was unlucky not to win the Derby. Only once in a hundred years does a horse secure a long uninterrupted run right on the rails as Charlottown did. In fact I feel I might well have had first and second in the 1966 Derby as Lord Rosebery's General Gordon, who unfortunately broke a fetlock after winning the Chester Vase, was a really good colt, too; make no mistake about that.

Blue Peter's next race was the Two Thousand Guineas for which he started joint favourite at 5/1 with the Aga Khan's Dhoti. The distance was really too short for him but on a cold, squally afternoon he ran on strongly from the Dip to win by quite a comfortable half length from my other runner Admiral's Walk, ridden by Harry Wragg, with Fairstone close up third.

Blue Peter did not run again before the Derby for which he was a heavily backed favourite at 7/2. A number of people opposed him on the grounds that

Fairway was unlikely to sire a stayer, which was curious in view of the fact that Fairway had won not only the St. Leger, but the two and a quarter mile Jockey Club Cup. Perhaps more reasonable grounds for opposition was the Stefan the Great blood close up in Blue Peter's pedigree. Among those who summed up against him was Bob Lyle of *The Times*. His column on the morning after the Derby began with a single word sentence—'Peccavi'.

It was a wonderful June afternoon for the Derby and the sun blazed down from a cloudless blue sky. The crowd was enormous and for a short time at least people forgot the dreadful tension of the international situation. Despite the heat Blue Peter remained wonderfully cool—cooler in fact than his owner and trainer—and in the parade there was nothing more than a faint mark of sweat where the reins touched his neck. I watched the race from the trainers' stand and there is honestly very little I can say about it except that I never felt worried. Approaching Tattenham Corner Eph Smith had Blue Peter perfectly placed as he was close up third behind Larchfield and Heliopolis. Early in the straight Larchfield was beaten and with three furlongs to go Blue Peter moved up to challenge Heliopolis. For a few strides Heliopolis seemed to be holding my horse but then Eph showed Blue Peter the whip and the result was both instantaneous and conclusive. Blue Peter immediately lengthened his stride and drew clear to win in majestic fashion amid tremendous cheering, from Fox Cub, whom Fred Darling trained for Mr. Esmond, and Heliopolis. Blue Peter had won like the champion he undoubtedly was and the crowd gave him and Lord Rosebery a terrific reception, in the course of which Lord Rosebery's allegedly stiff collar seemed to dissolve altogether. This was certainly one of the great moments of my life.

Some modern trainers strike me as gloomy fellows and they would hardly stand their best friend a drink after winning the Derby. Personally I rather enjoy a celebration. I used to go to the Piccadilly Hotel a lot in those days and I had a standing arrangement there that if ever I won the Derby they were to make arrangements for a dinner party for at least twenty people. I told my friends of this arrangement, too, and they rallied in force. Four of them heard the Derby result at Newmarket, changed into evening clothes and headed for London forthwith. We had a wonderful evening. In the party were Gwen Carlow, who later married Noel Murless, and George Greenwood who became Chairman of Kempton. I gave a party, too, at Newmarket for the members of the Subscription Rooms and another at the White Hart for my staff. There was, too, an expedition to Hunstanton for members of my staff with wives and sweethearts and I still have the telegram from Hunstanton dated the 6th of July 1939 and signed by my Head Man, Percy Double. 'Seventy-three persons thank you for your kindness and wish you good health and further successes.'

Lord Rosebery himself gave a marvellous party at the Savoy, just about the best I have ever been to. It had given me particular pleasure to win the Derby for Lord Rosebery. He has always honoured me with his complete confidence and when things go wrong he is a wonderful loser. He really does understand about racing and therefore avoids doing the silly things that some owners are occasionally inclined to to. He very rarely enters a horse himself, leaving that side of it entirely to me, but he did enter Ribbon for the Middle Park Stakes, which she duly won, defeating the famous Nasrullah.

Blue Peter's next race was the Eclipse Stakes at Sandown in which he started at 7/2 on. The St. Leger winner Scottish Union was judged to be the pick of the opposition but in fact Mr. Rank's horse ran poorly. Blue Peter won by a length and a half from Glen Loan and some people expressed disappointment that he had failed to spreadeagle his field. As a matter of fact Blue Peter ran a lazy sort of race; so much so that Eph Smith had to give him a sharp reminder with the whip. This woke the big chestnut up and he galloped on down to the Eclipse starting gate before Eph could pull him up.

I now prepared Blue Peter for the St. Leger and extraordinary interest was created by the prospect of a clash between him and M. Boussac's colt Pharis, who had won the French Derby and the Grand Prix, and like Blue Peter, was undefeated that season. I have no doubts at all in my own mind that Blue Peter would have beaten Pharis. Furthermore I take leave to question whether Pharis would ever have taken the field at Doncaster. The going was firm that autumn and on account of his conformation Pharis was hardly suited to a severe race on hard ground.

In any case I feel sure we would have beaten him and I base my opinion on a wonderful gallop that Blue Peter did. Tricameron, second to Pharis in the

77

Grand Prix, had beaten my horse Flyon at Chester so I decided to get a line on Pharis through Flyon. The gallop took place over a mile and three quarters of the Summer Gallop and resulted as follows:

1	Blue Peter	3 y o	9st. 5
2	Flyon	4 y o	9st. 5
3	Tutor	3 y o	7st. 5
4	Challenge	4 y o	9st. 5
5	Broconteur	3 y o	6st. 5
6	Foxlair II	3 y o	6st. 5

Won by six lengths; the same; others beaten off.

Bob Jewitt, a good judge whose father trained the mighty Isinglass, watched the gallop with me. 'The best gallop I ever saw,' he said. I myself had always thought Blue Peter to be very good indeed, but not till this gallop had I really appreciated what a magnificent stayer he was. I had told the boys on Broconteur and Foxlair II to come along at a good gallop and the others to 'ride a race'. After a mile Broconteur and Foxlair II were done with. With two furlongs to go Blue Peter and Flyon were left in front of Tutor who was tiring. Soon afterwards it was clear that Flyon was under pressure while Blue Peter was still pulling double. I pulled out my handkerchief and waved Smith on. The result was astonishing; Blue Peter sprinted away from Flyon as if he had only just started.

I had some really good trial horses that day. Flyon had won the Ascot Gold Cup by five lengths. Tutor had won four of his six races and was beaten a head in another. Challenge had been beaten a neck in the

St. Leger the year before and had won the Jockey Club Stakes; after the trial he beat French Derby winner, Cillas, at Newbury. Broconteur and Foxlair II were admittedly moderate, but the former had been placed four times in six starts, while Foxlair II was three times second.

Tutor had been bought to act as lead horse for Blue Peter. He then had the unattractive name of Loup Pendu, which Lord Rosebery changed, in view of his function, to Tutor. Later that year Tutor won the Manchester November Handicap by four lengths carrying 8st. 3, which represents Blue Peter at 10st. 13!

War, long expected, broke out in September and Doncaster was abandoned. Lord Rosebery had hoped to keep Blue Peter in training as a four-year-old to win the Ascot Gold Cup but in view of the uncertainty over racing's future, he decided to return him to the stud forthwith. I was very disappointed that Blue Peter was robbed by Hitler of his opportunity to win the 'Triple Crown'. I am sure he was superior to Bahram, the last horse to gain that distinction. Bahram never had a good horse to beat and some of his victories were far from impressive. Blue Peter was not the success as a sire that his many admirers anticipated. He certainly was not a failure, but in view of his outstanding merit he hardly came up to expectations. He made a wonderful start with Ocean Swell, winner of the Derby and the Gold Cup, but he never got another classic winner. Other notable winners by him were Botticelli (Gold Cup), Peter Flower (Hardwicke Stakes) and the unbeaten but unsound Blue Train who was out of the brilliant Sun Chariot. His

79

mares did well and he was leading sire of brood-mares in 1954. He died in 1957. It is only once in a lifetime that one can hope to train a horse as good as him.

I always think that Lord Rosebery ought to have won the 1931 Derby with Sandwich, a colt bred by Mr. J. J. Maher, by Sansovino out of Waffles and thus a half-brother to the dual classic winner Manna. Sandwich, whom Lord Rosebery bought for 3,600 guineas as a yearling, took plenty of time to come to hand. As a two-year-old he only ran once and then in inconspicuous fashion. The following season he was quite unfancied and down the course in the Craven Stakes and the Two Thousand Guineas. It was a different matter, though, when he came to racing over a longer distance and he won the mile and a half Chester Vase quite impressively.

On the strength of that Chester victory he started second favourite at 8/1 in the Derby. Unfortunately the race was not one of the happiest efforts of that very patient rider, Harry Wragg. Sandwich was soon in a very bad position and even at Tattenham Corner he was at the tail end of the field and in an apparently hopeless situation. It was only close home that he suddenly emerged from nowhere travelling twice as fast as anything else in the race. For a few seconds I thought he might just pull it off, but his effort had come too late and in the end he was third, beaten three parts of a length and the same, by Cameronian and Orpen. I have only seen one Derby loser as unlucky and that was Shantung who was third to Parthia in 1959. Sandwich would undoubtedly have won quite decisively in another hundred yards. After the race Wragg stated to the press 'It is possible I was an

Eph Smith, who rode Blue Peter to victory in the Derby shows
early promise in the saddle!

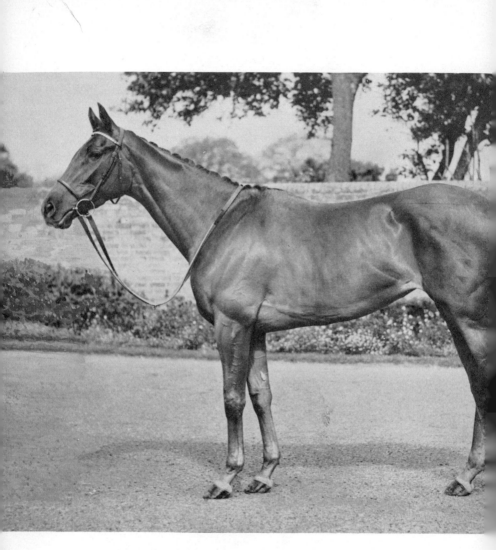

Mr David Wills's Happy Laughter—winner of the One Thousand
Guineas, a very game filly that triumphed over ill-health.

unlucky loser'. This observation struck some people as the understatement of the year.

Sandwich won the King Edward VII Stakes at Ascot and ran well to finish third in the Eclipse over a distance all too short for him. He was at his best for the St. Leger which he won in magnificent style by four lengths from Orpen. Cameronian ran an extraordinary race and finished last. Sandwich was a disappointment the following season and did not win a race apart from a walkover in 'The Whip'. He ran pretty well in the Cesarewitch, though, to finish third to a good mare in Nitsichin with 9st. 5 on his back. Unfortunately he proved a failure as a sire.

It was soon after Sandwich's St. Leger victory that I purchased some land at Newmarket from Mr. E. C. Rush and formed the Sandwich Stud. In old Lord Rosebery's day the mares were kept at Mentmore, where the ground is clay, and the yearlings went to the Durdans where the soil is chalk. On Lord Rosebery's death, the Durdans became the property of his daughter, Lady Sybil Grant, and the yearlings could no longer go there. The Sandwich Stud seemed a suitable place for the yearlings to be reared and Lord Rosebery agreed to become part-owner. After the war we sold the stud at a satisfactory price to Mr. Wilfred Harvey. Amongst the horses reared there were Blue Peter, Ocean Swell, Midas, Hyperides, Ribbon and Afterthought, all winners of Classics or placed in Classic events.

Another good horse of Lord Rosebery's at this period was Miracle, who was bred by Lord Beaverbrook and whom Lord Rosebery was able to purchase for the absurdly small price of 170 guineas. No doubt

81

a good many people thought that Miracle, a big over-grown baby with lop ears, would never stand training and he certainly bore no resemblance to his neat, dapper sire, Manna. Miracle, however, gradually developed strength and he made a highly satisfactory first appearance at Goodwood, winning the Selsey Stakes. He only ran once again that season and won the Gimcrack Stakes at York. In the Free Handicap he was given 8st. 13, 8lbs. less than the top weight Orwell.

When I first saw Miracle I said he would either be very good or very bad. As a three-year-old he proved himself beyond argument to be very good. He won the Newmarket Stakes and was then third in the Derby to April the Fifth and Dastur. In the Derby I also ran Royal Dancer, owned by Mr. Esmond and ridden by Sam Wragg, who finished fourth. It was unfortunate that the brothers Wragg both went for the same opening simultaneously and collided. Both stated confidently afterwards that they would have won but for that regrettable contretemps. I ran Miracle in the Prince of Wales's Stakes at Royal Ascot but he was no doubt still feeling the effects of his Epsom exertions and starting at 7/4 on in a field of five, he was well beaten by Victor Gilpin's Sigiri to whom he was conceding 12lbs. Miracle's best performance was to win the Eclipse Stakes very easily indeed in a strong field of thirteen. He finished five lengths in front of Firdaussi, who subsequently won the St. Leger. I feel sure Miracle would have won that race, but unfortunately he broke down a week before Doncaster. I rang up and told Lord Rosebery of the mishap which was affecting his back tendon.

Lord Rosebery ordered me to wire and strike Miracle out of the St. Leger at once in case any members of the public should back him and not get a run for their money. Miracle never ran again and proved very disappointing at the stud.

Before leaving this epoch I must relate a story about a very nice chap called Mitchell who came over to Newmarket with the American horse Reigh Count. Before the Royal Ascot meeting we told Mitchell that he could not possibly let the Newmarket trainers down and he would have to wear a top hat at the meeting. Mitchell resolutely refused on the grounds that he had never worn a top hat in his life and furthermore he did not intend to now. We pressed the point and at last he gave way. 'But,' he added, 'I guess it's going to be one of those collapsible bastards!'

CHAPTER VIII

In my opinion the best jockey is the one that wins the most races he is not really entitled to win. It is largely for that reason that I rate American-born Danny Maher as the finest rider of my experience.

The so-called 'American Invasion' of the English turf at the turn of the century revolutionised race-riding over here. The streamlined American style, embodying short leathers and the forward seat, rapidly supplanted the traditional English method which was elegant enough when performed by experts, but of course offered the maximum wind resistance. English jockeys simply had to pull up their leathers or get out of the game. Mornington Cannon, a great horseman and a beautiful rider of the old school, declined to adapt himself to change and gradually drifted out of racing. Another very fine rider of the old school, Jack Watts—he rode four Derby winners—was my godfather, after whom I was named. I well remember going to Jack Watts's house, recently demolished, on the day of Queen Victoria's Diamond Jubilee to watch a balloon ascend from the end of the Heath just where the Old Portland Stand used to be. A passenger in the balloon was Major Osmund Griffiths, whose son used to conduct auctions at Newmarket meetings until selling races were abolished there. I recollect that Major Griffiths was instructed by the 'captain' of the balloon to grip the ropes hard and pull himself off his feet when the balloon touched down to prevent any risk of breaking his legs.

The American riders were laughed at to begin with but before long their astonishing successes wiped the smile off the faces of their critics. The first of them was a coloured rider called Simms, who never really made good. He was followed by Tod Sloan, the Reiff brothers, Lester and Johnny, 'Skeets' Martin and Danny Maher. Tod Sloan was an erratic character and did not last long over here, but he nevertheless altered the whole style of English riding. He used an exaggerated crouch and actually rode with his knees over the saddle flaps. I always tended to regard him rather in the light of a riding freak, but at his best he was very good and he was undoubtedly a fine judge of pace. He may well, however, have been flattered by the advantage he derived from his stream-lined style at a time when only a few English riders had changed their methods.

To revert to Danny Maher, he seemed to combine some of the grace of the old style with the effectiveness of the new. He had a beautiful seat on a horse and wonderful hands. No one could balance a horse more perfectly for a challenge and his sense of timing was uncanny. He was a man of great charm and when, before the 1913 Derby, old Lord Rosebery expressed his willingness to release him from riding his little-fancied filly Prue, Maher felt strongly that he ought to honour his retainer and turned down an offer to ride the favourite, Craganour. His conduct makes an interesting and highly favourable comparison with the attitude of certain other leading jockeys in similar circumstances.

Unfortunately Maher died all too young of tuberculosis. The riders that in my opinion have approximated most closely to him were Charlie Elliott and the late 'Manny' Mercer. Born in Durham, 'Manny' was a most engaging personality and a natural rider. He had the best of hands and horses went well for him. But for his tragic death as the result of an accident at Ascot, I am convinced he would have reached the very top of the tree.

Charlie Elliott was a wonderful rider at his peak. The son of Lord George Dundas's travelling head lad, he came to me as a boy and I taught him to ride. Seldom can a boy have made swifter progress. The season after he had ridden his first winner, he became my stable jockey and rode Golden Myth to victory in the Gold Vase, the Gold Cup and the Eclipse Stakes. I think the finest races he ever rode were towards the end of his career on Souepi in the Gold Cup and the Goodwood Cup. In both those races he was second one stride before the post and one stride after it, but he was in front as he actually passed it.

Charlie Elliott was still apprenticed to me when he deposed Steve Donoghue from the position of Champion Jockey in 1924, a position that Steve had occupied for the previous ten years. In 1923 he had shared the lead with Steve, both of them riding eighty-nine winners. He won the Derby on Call Boy, Bois Roussel and Nimbus, there being a gap of twenty-two years between his first Derby winner and his last one. Nimbus was a fine big bay colt by Nearco and was trained by George Colling for Mrs. Glenister, the wife of an official of the Midland Bank. It so happened that George Colling was ill when the Derby was run and he asked me to saddle Nimbus for him. When I went down to the paddock I found Nimbus standing still in the centre of it with a distinctly apprehensive small boy on his back. Nimbus was obviously very much on edge, kicking, sweating, and refusing to move. George's head lad was there, too, and so were Mr. and Mrs. Glenister and George's wife. I told the boy to dismount and I then got Nimbus to walk quietly down to the saddling stalls that used to stand up against the fence dividing the paddock from the Durdans. There we dried Nimbus off and settled him down.

Unfortunately, just as a somewhat tricky situation was beginning to look a bit more promising, along came Noel Murless with the Derby favourite, Royal Forest, accompanied by a throng of spectators who wanted to see the favourite saddled. I did not want Nimbus to get hotted up again so I decided to get him into the parade ring forthwith. George had given orders that the boy was to ride him round but I was convinced that Nimbus was very much happier without the boy on his back. Accordingly I told the boy to walk along in readiness in case he was needed but not to mount him. This was not an easy decision for me to make as it was contrary to George's orders and if Nimbus, a high-mettled colt like many of his sire's stock, had played up and got loose, I should have had to carry the blame. It would certainly have been impossible for the head lad to make a similar decision. Luckily everything went well and after a thrilling race Nimbus won by a head from Amour Drake with Swallow Tail only a head away third. It was the first Derby in which the verdict was decided by the camera. Incidentally I never received a word of thanks from Mrs. Glenister or her husband. I am convinced that but for the action I took Nimbus would have taken the race out of himself before going to the post.

Earlier in this chapter I mentioned Craganour, the favourite for the 1913 Derby. As is well known Craganour passed the post first only to be disqualified by the Stewards on the grounds that he had not kept a straight course and had interfered with Shogun, Day Comet and Aboyeur; furthermore that he had bumped and bored Aboyeur, the 100/1 outsider who was awarded the race.

I watched this race from the top of the stand just by George Duller's father, old 'Hoppy' Duller. Aboyeur was in front at Tattenham Corner with Craganour close up on his outside. Aboyeur swung a little bit wide at the bend and soon afterwards Frank Wootton brought Shogun up with the obvious intention of going through the narrow gap between Aboyeur and the rails. At that point I believe that Johnny Reiff, who was riding Craganour, shouted to Piper on Aboyeur to close the gap. Piper took no action, whereupon Reiff bored in on Aboyeur who in his turn veered towards the rails, hampering Shogun who was going very well at the time and may have been a very unlucky loser.

Aboyeur did not take all this lying down and from then on right up to the winning post it was a barging match between the favourite and Aboyeur. It was Reiff on Craganour, though, who started the trouble and I have always been emphatic that the decision of the Stewards to disqualify Craganour was the right one. From what I had seen with my own eyes I was sure that Craganour would lose the race, and pausing only to bet 'Hoppy' Duller a fiver that there would be an objection, I went down to the Ring to have a wager. The bookmakers took the view that there was little danger of the favourite losing the race and were laying long odds against Aboyeur, whom they were only too glad to get into their books at all. This suited me, and my confidence in the outcome was increased when I met George Stern, who had ridden Great Sport, ultimately placed third, in the passage leading from the stewards' room. 'They're going to disqualify that bloody horse,' observed George; which in due course they did and I won £5,000 in bets, a very nice sum for a young man in those days.

George Stern was an Englishman who rode mostly in France. He was not only a very good rider indeed, exceptionally strong in a finish, but an extremely tough one, too, and if there was any funny business in a race, it was highly improbable that he would emerge second best. Sometimes his tactics were unorthodox to say the very least and he rode a dreadfully rough race on the French horse Eider that dead-heated with The White Knight in the Ascot Gold Cup. Inevitably Eider was disqualified. It was not infrequently alleged that when Stern was getting the worse of a tight finish, he was not above gripping his rival jockey by the knee.

In appearance Stern was short, broad-shouldered,

almost thick-set in fact, and immensely powerful. As far as looks went he reminded me rather of the steeplechase jockey Alf Newey. I always reckon that Newey's feat in riding Eremon to victory in the 1907 Grand National after breaking a stirrup leather at the second fence was one of the finest and pluckiest bits of riding I have ever seen. When Newey came into the weighing room after the race, the inside of his thighs were bleeding where they had been so badly chafed. Another great piece of riding in the Grand National was by Bruce Hobbs on the little American horse Battleship in 1938. Over the last fence Battleship landed some three lengths behind that fine big Irish chaser, Royal Danieli. Bruce took up his whip but Battleship obviously did not like it and he at once put it down. He then rode Battleship right up that long run-in to the winning post with his hands, Battleship getting his head in front in the final stride to win by inches. Bruce was only seventeen years of age at the time, and bearing in mind that fact and that so much was at stake, the temptation to use his whip must have been almost overpowering.

Of course I always had the utmost admiration for Gordon Richards and no man has lost fewer races that he ought to have won. His style was unique and quite inimitable. At times he seemed to be leaning so far to one side that it looked any odds on the horse becoming unbalanced, but in fact that never seemed to happen. His consistency, integrity and his will to win made him the best friend the English punter has ever had. I have met people who thought Bernard Carslake the finest rider they have ever seen but in my opinion it was a grave disadvantage that he could only use his whip with one hand. I am inclined to rate Frank Bullock the best of the many good Australian riders that have come over here. Frank Wootton could be very effective, but to compare him with Danny Maher was like comparing a T-model Ford with a Rolls-Royce; they both got you there in the end, but you had a far better ride in the Rolls. Most Australian jockeys improve immensely after they have been over here for a bit and have got thoroughly acclimatised to English racing. That certainly applied both to Scobie Breasley and Ron Hutchinson. In my dealings with Australian riders I always find them very polite and business-like; they are frequently more clued-up and sophisticated, not least over money matters, than their English counterparts. I have seldom met a nicer or better mannered boy than the young South African, John Gorton, who rode over here in the autumn of 1966. I admire Lester Piggott but frankly my admiration is qualified by various factors. Firstly I am inclined to think there is not a great level of competition nowadays and that the general level of jockeyship is far lower than it was, say, between the wars. Secondly I think he rides ludicrously short. Certainly his style, with his bottom stuck up in the air, is the reverse of elegant and it is a pity that some young riders try to copy it. In my own riding days I was above all taught to keep my hands down and never to turn round. Far too many modern riders, Piggott included, are apt to turn round and by so doing they unbalance their mounts.

Piggott came to my stable in 1954 after he had lost

his licence following incidents in the King Edward VII Stakes at Royal Ascot when he was riding the Derby winner, Never Say Die. The Stewards of the Jockey Club thought it would do him good to be away from home for a bit and his father asked me to take him. This I gladly did, and he 'did his two' and rode out for me. We got on quite well; he certainly never gave me cause to complain and I know I was instrumental in getting his licence restored earlier than otherwise it would have been.

Eph Smith rode for me for many years and a very good, dependable rider he was, too. Many jockeys in this country come from working-class homes in industrial areas but Eph and his brother Doug are sons of a Berkshire farmer. They were brought up with animals and Eph first attracted attention as a very small boy by his prowess on a jumping donkey. Bill Rickaby has the advantages of family tradition and education, but though he rode many good races for me, he was almost too modest and diffident by nature and on big occasions inclined to lack self-confidence, a weakness no one could ever have accused Charlie Smirke of sharing. I am happy to record that Bill rode his final winner on a horse I trained, Silver Spray, and the wonderful reception Bill received was a tribute to the affection felt for him by the racing public. I thought Steve Donoghue was rather overrated and I did not admire him as a man either. Harry Wragg rode many good races for me but sometimes he overdid the waiting tactics and I shall always think that he ought to have won the 1931 Derby on Sandwich.

In some respects the business of training horses

has become more difficult since I first came into racing. In those pre-motor-car days, we all depended on the horse far more for transport and the horse was all-important both in agriculture and in the army as well. Many stable lads had had previous experience of horses, not thoroughbreds of course, before a trainer took them on, whereas in this present mechanical age they nearly all have to start from scratch. I think Irish trainers perhaps have the edge on us in this respect as Ireland is an agricultural country rather than an industrial one like England and many Irish stable employees have had experience with animals of some sort even if not with horses. The modern stable lad is apt not to know his job thoroughly, let alone feel any sense of dedication towards it. Too many of them are inveterate clock-watchers, but happily there is a percentage who take an interest and do their best. Because of the conditions of employment existing today, horses tend to go out for shorter and shorter periods and this of course is to their detriment. It is not too much to say that some horses never get properly trained. Speaking for myself, I refuse to give in to the practice of sending horses out for insufficient periods and this does not render my own labour problems any easier.

In the old days horses used to do a lot of road-work in the winter which was undoubtedly good for their legs, but the immense amount of traffic nowadays renders this virtually impossible, the position being aggravated by the fact that many drivers show no consideration whatsoever to horses and their riders. Before we all had cars, the racing world was a far more closely-knit community than it is now and the members of it knew each other better. We were constantly travelling on trains together and staying overnight in the same hotels. Of course it was in many respects inconvenient not getting home in the evening, but looking back on it all, we did manage to have a lot of fun.

I was Chairman of the Trainers Federation when stablemen were first being recruited into the Transport and General Workers Union, the boss of which was then the formidable Mr. Ernest Bevin. The situation at the time was far from easy as certain trainers resolutely declined to recognise the Union at all. Fortunately old Lord Derby stepped in and it was arranged that under his chairmanship a deputation of trainers should meet Union officials. George Lambton, Tommy Hogg and I met Bevin at Transport House. We found him most sympathetic and easy to talk to and he fully realised the difficulty of applying trade union hours where the maintenance of live-stock was concerned. I remember at one stage he was talking of his early life and the shock I felt when he said 'and then I became an agitator'. Agitator or not, he was extremely fair to us trainers.

I had the greatest respect for old Lord Derby. I felt it was a great privilege when my advice was asked for as regards a successor to take over from George Lambton and it was on my recommendation that Colledge Leader was appointed as Derby's trainer at the end of 1933. He was a very fine trainer indeed and it was a tragedy that he died only a few years later.

There seems no limit to the ever-rising costs that trainers have to face and of course training fees have risen enormously, too, though even now they are hardly realistic in view of the overheads that have to be met. I have a letter written to me during the First World War by Lord Harewood, grandfather of the present peer, in which he says that the conditions which the Government were planning to impose in respect of racing would make owners most reluctant to pay a weekly training fee of 60/-! The time may not be far off when the usual fee will be £20 per week per horse. Unfortunately prize money has not risen in the same proportion.

Among the greatest trainers I have known were Charles Morton, Alec Taylor, Richard Marsh, Fred Darling and Frank Butters. Unlike some modern trainers, Morton had had a thorough grounding before he started training and what he did not know about horses' legs was not worth the bother of learning. He was a professional in the very best sense of that word. His finest feat was to win the Derby with Mr. Jack Joel's Sunstar who had really broken down a fortnight before the Epsom Summer meeting began. At any rate Sunstar had strained a suspensory ligament so badly that he could barely put his foot to the ground. Somehow or other Morton managed to get Sunstar, who had been heavily backed by the public, to the post though he warned Mr. Joel that the colt would never be able to race again afterwards. Sunstar duly won, but he was terribly lame on his return to the unsaddling enclosure and as Morton had said, he never saw a racecourse again.

Richard Marsh, a great horseman in his day and always beautifully dressed, trained four Derby winners, and his greatest achievement in my opinion was

95

to win the 1909 Derby with Minoru who came out early in the season and won the Greenham Stakes at Newbury under 9st. 10, much to the surprise of the King's racing manager Lord Marcus Beresford who had remarked in the paddock, 'He's certainly improved, but 7st. 4 in the Stewards Cup is more his class!' Minoru next won the Two Thousand Guineas and the critics were unanimous that Marsh had got him to his peak too soon and that he was bound to be stale by Derby Day. Minoru, in fact, looked magnificent at Epsom and won a terrific race by the shortest of heads from Mr. Walter Raphael's Louviers. This was followed by one of the most extraordinary scenes I have ever known. The King went down and out to the course to lead his hope in. The crowd surged round him cheering and throwing their hats in the air. I remember seeing an old boxing character, Jimmy Carney, his hat gone and red in the face, helping to keep the crowd back from the King.

I got to know some of the American trainers who came to Newmarket at the time of the 'American Invasion'. John Huggins, trained Volodyovski to win the Derby in 1901. He was always very kind to me when I was a boy and sometimes used to give me a golden sovereign which he extracted from his sovereign purse. When I went back to school after the holidays I rode a horse of his in the Great Surrey Handicap at Epsom, and kind as he invariably was, he was most concerned that I should come to no harm. He was undoubtedly a first-class man at his job. Another good American trainer was Andrew Joyner who, like Huggins, used to run his horses in the most straightforward manner imaginable. He was

96

exceptionally popular at Newmarket and the trainers there gave him a big dinner on the eve of his return to the United States. Wishard was another American trainer of first rate ability, but there is no doubt at all that he went in for doping. He had brought over the Reiff brothers with him. Lester Reiff was tall and had a lot of trouble with his weight. He worked very closely with certain American gamblers over here and if certain of these gamblers did not back a short priced favourite that he rode, then that favourite was destined not to win. Johnny Reiff first appeared on English courses looking the picture of innocence in a knickerbocker suit and an Eton collar, but he was a good deal more worldly-wise than his appearance suggested. He won the Derby in 1907 on Orby and again 1912 on Tagalie.

There is no doubt that in modern times doping and nobbling do occur occasionally, but I think the whole subject has been greatly exaggerated. Until recently the Jockey Club handled the situation very clumsily, and very unfairly too, making no differentiation between horses doped to win and those that had been nobbled to ensure them losing. In either case a positive test could result in the trainer losing his licence, regardless of the fact that no trainer, unless bereft of his senses, would stop a horse of his own from winning by giving it dope. After all, there are easier ways of killing a cat than choking it to death with cream. Because of the Jockey Club ruling, a trainer was naturally reluctant ever to have a horse officially tested as a positive result might result in the loss of his livelihood. A filly of Lord Rosebery's called Snap was privately tested and the result was positive, it being apparently found that the elements of two different drugs were present in extremely small quantities. There was a certain lapse of time before the test was taken after Snap had run at Newmarket and personally I always entertain doubts as to whether in fact she was really nobbled. A lot of money is expended on stable and racecourse security nowadays and I only hope it is money well spent. At the Epsom racecourse stables the security guards were nearly driven insane one night by the activities of an owl who kept on flying through an electric beam which each time set off the alarms.

It is sometimes alleged that our horses are not as tough and robust as they were and do not stand up to hard work and hard racing like they used to. I have not found that to be the case myself, but of course it is impossible really to generalise about horses. Each one has its own individuality and it is pointless trying to treat them all alike. Some need a lot of work, others practically none at all. The art of training lies largely in assessing correctly the characteristics, capabilities and requirements of individual horses. I attribute our lack of success in big races in recent years primarily to the lack of prepotent classic sires such as Cyllene, Gainsborough, Blandford, Fairway, Hyperion and Nearco. I think the late Aga Khan, who had derived immense benefits from English racing, did the sport lamentable disservice by letting his stallions go overseas. It would have been a different and happier story if Blenheim, Bahram, Mahmoud and Nasrullah had stayed in this country or in Ireland. In fairness to the Aga Khan, he did not export Nasrullah himself to America; he sold him to

Mr. J. McGrath who later re-sold him. Moreover purely on Nasrullah's racing career it was difficult to foresee his brilliant success as a stallion. He never gave the impression of being very fond of the game after Lord Rosebery's filly Ribbon beat him in a terrific race for the Middle Park Stakes.

CHAPTER IX

One of the most controversial events in racing during the nineteen-twenties was the match at Belmont Park, U.S.A., in 1923 between the American horse Zev and the Derby winner Papyrus, owned by Mr. Ben Irish, and trained by my brother Basil.

The original intention of the match, which was thought up in New York by the Westchester Racing Association, was to boost racing there and stimulate public interest. In general there was far less interest taken by the general American public in racing than is taken by the public over here, perhaps because of the lack of off-course betting facilities. The head of the Westchester Association was Mr. August Belmont, a much respected man who had bought the 'Triple Crown' winner Rock Sand and who had won the St. Leger with Rock Sand's son Tracery, who in his turn was sire of Papyrus.

After Papyrus had been beaten, there were some scathing criticisms about the match which some people closely connected with racing erroneously thought was a ridiculous farce that had brought little credit to England or to the English Turf. Furthermore, there was an inference, wholly false,

100

that the connections of Papyrus had been motivated in the affair primarily, if not solely, by financial considerations. In reality, the fact that Papyrus, with the cards clearly stacked against him, had taken up the challenge and 'had a go', did this country quite a bit of good. To try to put the record straight I should like to give my brother Basil's account of the whole affair.

By Basil Jarvis (trainer of Papyrus)
For several reasons, but for one in particular, I have not hesitated to write here the true story of the facts leading up to the sending of Papyrus to America to race against the best three-year-old in that country, at the same time giving some intimate details of the voyage, the short period of training, and the actual race itself. I believe some of my countrymen and women will be glad of the details I can now unfold, but primarily, it will enable me to rebut the seriously damaging suggestions made in the press and elsewhere that this adventure with the English Derby winner of 1923 was not made in the true interests of sport but merely for sordid purposes. I feel it is due to Mr. Irish, as the owner of Papyrus, to myself as his trainer, and to the American people to do something to check the unfair, most unkind, and ungenerous way the whole thing has been dealt with by the English Press, with about one notable exception. I find on my return that malign suggestions have been made against us after we set out with the horse, and this is the first opportunity that has been offered of saying anything in reply. One sporting newspaper has described the incident as a travesty of sport which had

best be forgotten. The point of view of the paper is notoriously narrow at all times, but in this case it has chosen to condemn while preferring to remain in ignorance of the facts. Another paper has said that in future our politicians and horses should be kept at home. I have not the slightest doubt that the visit of Papyrus to America, though futile in itself, has done more for the betterment of relations between the two countries than that paper will ever do by insolent innuendo of that kind. We have been beaten before in sport in the United States, but never before has defeat brought in its trail a higher admiration of the sportsmanship of the Englishmen, both in regard to their scrupulously fair methods and their way of accepting bad luck, involving as it did the extinguishing at the eleventh hour of any hopes of success.

When the idea was first launched of sending Papyrus to America, I never dreamed of all that was to be associated with it in an international sense. My vision limited itself to a match between two horses without sensing the remarkable way America would come to interest herself. During the Goodwood meeting, at the end of July last, the Military Attaché connected with the United States Embassy in London introduced himself to me, and mentioned that he had been requested to sound me as to the possibilities of Papyrus visiting America in the autumn to run against the best of their three-year-olds for a prize of 100,000 dollars. My first ideas were that the prize to the winner was to be £25,000, with £5,000 to the owner of the beaten horse. As a matter of fact it turned out that the sum of 100,000 dollars was to be inclusive of the consolation prize of £5,000.

The idea attracted me from the outset. I knew that Papyrus, if Mr. Irish held to his present intentions, was not likely to be kept in training after his three-year-old days, while the proposed match would not interfere with the programme to run him for the St. Leger, for which, as the Derby winner, I naturally fancied him very much. My first move was to consult Mr. Irish, who was at once interested, though neither of us quite figured out at the moment how inadequate the £5,000 was likely to be in covering transport, the jockey's fee, insurance, my own expenses, compensating for partial loss of the autumn racing season at home, and no end of other expenses. They simply grew and grew, but at the time we did not realise how much. I mention this in order to take an opportunity thus early to refute any suggestion that Mr. Irish was to get a lot of money out of sending his horse to America on a wild goose chase.

The next move was a cable to Mr. August Belmont asking whether expenses would be guaranteed in the event of either horse being unable to run through going wrong. Mr. Belmont replied: 'We are delighted with your general acceptance which we confirm as satisfactory to us. Pending arranging details we submit for your choice any Saturday up to and including October 20th.' Apparently October 20th was the last date available and we chose that in order to give us as long an interval as possible between landing and the race. We had in mind at the time shipping the horse on the Leviathan on September 18th. As a matter of fact he did not sail until four days later, namely the 22nd, on the Cunarder, Aquitania.

The question of conceding the rights of taking the pictures for the cinema cropped up very soon afterwards. I can assure you that it had not been thought of by either Mr. Irish or myself up to then, and, meanwhile we had practically committed ourselves to the venture. Yet it has been suggested throughout that this match was arranged solely in the interests of the cinema out of which we were to receive huge profits. We have been accused of sordid commercialism and all that sort of thing. I repeat that the point never arose until Mr. Irish had accepted the suggestions from America, with only £5,000 from America to rely on with which to pay those serving him in the event of the colt being unsuccessful.

I take it that in these days the film business necessarily tacks itself on to any subject of national or international interest, and soon after the match had been ratified we were approached with the view to conceding the rights. As a business matter any rights to which we felt entitled to were shared. What small percentage was retained by Mr. Irish, who found himself committed to big expenses in order to send me to America and to secure the services of Donoghue, was not likely to reimburse him, and, therefore, I say now that as the loser in the match he will be lucky if he makes both ends meet. It would, of course, have been otherwise had he won with Papyrus.

I have not the faintest shadow of doubt that Mr. Belmont and the members of the American Jockey Club were actuated by sporting motives in bringing about the race, and from the outset, right up to the end, I never had cause to waver in that view, indeed it increased. After all their enterprise, organisation, risk and trouble I do not think they would clear as much profit as accrues from a single day's racing at one of our big meetings. Again, in regard to Mr. Irish, let me say that he had to meet the heavy insurance expenses, for his horse was insured for something like £40,000.

I may appropriately begin my story of the events leading up to the actual race by detailing the colt's life on board the Aquitania from 21st to 29th of September. He had a wonderfully big box, and my idea was to let his lad get on his back each morning and evening, and keep him on the move round the box. It would not be much in the way of exercise, but it would be something. Then each morning and evening he was to be well massaged and wiped for an hour. But when a tremendous gale sprung up on the Monday these plans had to be altered. It really was awful weather with tremendous seas, one of which smashed the windows of the bridge room situated many feet above the sea. The lads fell ill and I followed suit. Yet the horse was fed, watered, and seen to, though the programme I have sketched could not be carried through for a day or two.

When the gale had blown itself out we had fair weather, and all I had planned for the horse was duly carried out. We had crowds of visitors, enormous interest being taken in him both by the 700 saloon passengers and the crew. At one time or another they must have all come to see him in the mornings or evenings, and the funniest questions were asked. One lady wanted to know if the boy was always on his back. Another wanted to know what he was going to America for, and when I said he was going to race she wanted to know what he was going to race against. She was most surprised when I told her he was going to race against another horse. Lots of people wanted to feed him oranges, bananas or nuts!

I must say in all my time I have never had to do with such an extraordinary horse. He seems almost human in his understanding of things, adapting himself to undreamed of situations as if he had been used to them all his life. His temperament and intelligence are simply beautiful, and no words of mine can convey what a glorious horse he is to do with. He is kindness and understanding itself, and, if he had not been, then I do not hesitate to say we should not have got him to the post at all. He would have been a dreadful anxiety, but as a horse he was no anxiety at all. A Christian if ever there was one! You simply have to love a horse like him, but then it is inconceivable that there is another like him, combining his racing qualities with his wonderful qualities of temperament.

Every day on board a bulletin was published about him and his welfare, and in a souvenir which was printed, the Captain, Sir James Charles, was supposed to send a letter to the horse in the course of which he is made to say—'I am sorry that the circumstances over which we have no control should have caused you new sensations and, I am afraid, some discomfort. There is, however, this satisfaction to be drawn from your adversity. You (including Bar Gold) have both shown a cheery gameness and lightheartedness which have won our unstinted admiration. True English sportsmen both of you. It only remains to wish you the best of luck in your gallant enterprise, and to tell you that, win or lose, we know that the proudest traditions of British sportsmanship will be worthily upheld by you.'

During the voyage he lost a little in condition, but then during the storm he did not feed. He picked up after that, and when he came to land he was in tolerably good condition. And what a landing it was! It astonished me. It was the first evidence I had of the immense public interest in the horse and the race among the people of New York. The dock was packed with folk, so also were the approaches to it, and the streets. As the horse was led down the gangway every deck of the liner was crowded and they cheered so much, both on the ship and the shore, that Papyrus was really frightened. I had to hold up my hand and in that way beg them to be quiet. They responded at once. The colt walked straight into a motor horse box without giving the slightest trouble and in that way we set out for Belmont Park, which was a journey of close on two hours. The streets were crowded and, while some motor police acted as an escort, others held up the traffic for us. So we did arrive at the end of our long journey.

First impressions are not likely to be easily effaced. Excellent stabling on the American plan had been prepared for us, though there is a vast difference from the well-ordered and finished appearance of an English training establishment. The boxes are all made of wood, and they have wooden floors. They all face to a covered ride, which is necessary in the winter when the weather is hard and the horses must be exercised within the shelter of the ride. The weather when we arrived on the 29th September was terribly hot and the flies were awful. We found means of defeating the fly scourge, but the heat really was trying for both ourselves and the horses.

Papyrus was quite fresh when we came to unload him from the motor box, but he was sweating a lot. However he soon settled down in his new quarters, and, after being done up, three Pinkerton police came on the scene to stand guard over him. From that time he was never left unguarded. The police were provided by the Racecourse Association; indeed no trouble was too big or too small for them to take.

One of the first things I did after seeing the horses comfortable was to walk on to the course on which the horse would have to do his work and race when the time came. I must say I got an awful shock. When I realised what the horse would have to gallop on I did not think I would ever get him to the post. The training ground consisted of the race-course itself, and a smaller track a mile in circumference. They were both terribly hard, what I will call the foundation being covered with about two inches of dirt—made up of a sort of dry dusty, grit and small stones. When they learned of my bitter disappointment at the state of the track I must say they did everything they possibly could to bring some improvement. They set about doing what they could, and the Belmont Trainers, including Andrew Joyner, afterwards told me that thanks to the coming of Papyrus they had never known such 'wonderful' going. What they must have had to put up with before goodness knows. If it was worse than I found it, well 'nuff said.

I may say here that I had to go slow with the horse at the outset, even though the time was so desperately short. He had been through a lot, and he had, of course, to be braced up for serious work. On the morning after his arrival I took him on to the track for an hour and a half, giving him trotting and walking exercise. It was then that I noticed the owner (Mr. Sinclair) and the trainer (Hildreth) of Zev first set eyes on him. I was at once absolutely pestered by visitors and Press. I must say here that the American Press were kindness itself to me throughout, but they were a little trying at first. I suppose they were just an index of the great public interest in the colt's arrival. Finally I got them to put in their papers that Papyrus could only be seen when out at exercise, and I had to lock the gates admitting to the stables. There was no trouble after that. On the Tuesday Papyrus did his first canters in America and apparently created a good impression. On returning to the stables there was a deputation of ten Pressmen waiting to be introduced and to interview me. On the following day after cantering a mile, Papyrus did not feed so well, and here I should say that from that time to the day of the race he did not feed up as he used to do in England. Probably he consumed 4lbs. less corn per day in America than he did in England. I knew from that he could not be the real Papyrus. I naturally put it down to the change of climate and conditions, and it is a matter which must be reckoned with in any other venture of this kind.

His first fast work was exactly a week after leaving the boat. He galloped a mile in 1 min. 47⅕ seconds, taking 5 seconds less to do the last quarter than the first quarter. He was now beginning to make a favourable impression on the American critics, who every morning came to the track. Then on 9th October occurred something which at the time made me feel quite certain there would be no match.

That morning he covered a mile at three-parts speed in 2 minutes 19 seconds before a large crowd. Mr. Foxhall Keene was one of those who came to see him work. He pulled up all right, but on going to stables in the evening we found heat in his near fore fetlock joint. The leg was also slightly filled. I had him brought out of his box, and there was no doubt about his lameness. He walked distinctly short. With the day of the race so near I did not see how he could possibly be right, especially as he would have to gallop on the track which had brought about the lameness.

Mr. Pride-Jones, the veterinary surgeon who had accompanied me from Newmarket, at once set about remedying the serious trouble, and so efficacious was his treatment that in twenty-four hours the heat and filling had disappeared. This was far better than we had thought possible. There was nothing for it but to push more work into him and so forty-eight hours after the lameness had been first discovered he was able to do a steady mile and a quarter. To my intense relief I saw him pull up sound and walk away no worse. That was an anxious day for us because all the day we were wondering how we should find him on going to him in the evening at stable time. However he was all right. It was almost past belief that it should have been so. No doubt given himself a blow.

On Saturday the 13th, exactly a week before the race, he covered a mile and a half in 2 mins. 38⅖ seconds. It was the first and only time he galloped a mile and a half between the St. Leger and this race in America. Bar Gold in this gallop carried a 6st. boy, lent by the trainer Mr. Welch. In all the circumstances it was a satisfactory gallop, and from this time American expert opinion was decidedly veering round in favour of Papyrus. It was not so, however, with a well-known English owner, who happened to be in New York at the time on a short visit. He did all he could to 'crab' the horse and the match. The American public could not understand it at all, and I do not exaggerate when I say that the views he allowed to be published made a very bad impression.

Papyrus continued to do well and make new friends. The climax may be said to have come when he showed something like his real self, when ridden by Donoghue over nine furlongs on the morning of the 18th, which was two days before the race. Still the weather was dry and warm, and the track, though it had been frequently harrowed and watered, remained its dry and dusty state. Papyrus, however, like the sensible horse he is was accustoming himself to it. Of that I am certain. That morning about a thousand spectators came to see the colt do his work, most of them having stop watches. Papyrus covered the nine furlongs in 1 min 50⅖ seconds, though Donoghue never for a moment extended him. It was just what we in England would call a good exercise gallop, and yet he had done time which was better than any put up by Zev. Anyhow, it so impressed the American critics, and I suppose they included some of the best judges of racing in the country, that they caused Papyrus to become favourite. That evening he was at a shade of odds on. I must say I shared the new hopes of him, and ventured to send Mr. Irish a cable telling him that in my opinion his horse held a 'good sporting chance of winning'.

Let there be no misunderstanding about it. It was American money that made the English horse favourite. On the day he started at even money, while Zev started at 10 to 9 on. So much for those in England who wrote and talked scoffingly of Papyrus having no earthly chance. What the Americans thought about him and the way they lost their money through backing their opinion is the best answer to those who have declared that Papyrus never had a dog's chance. That the horse was destined to be beaten was due to no fault of his. That we were made to appear apparently foolish by the result was due to no ridiculous miscalculation on our part. It was due to an absolutely unforeseen circumstance which could not possibly have been guarded against. I knew Papyrus was not the colt he was at Epsom or Doncaster, but even so I believed on the eve of the race that he would be good enought to do the task set him, and I should be untrue to my opinions and beliefs were I to think otherwise now.

Fortune turned her back on us on Friday morning when there came a distinct drop in the temperature. By the evening rain began to fall, the first rain after drought extending over weeks and months. It assumed the dimensions of a deluge, and for ten hours on end it never ceased. When I went on to the course on the morning of the race, it is impossible to convey in language the state I found it in. It was absolutely transformed, the water was lying on the surface

The late 'Manny' Mercer going out to win the National Breeders
Produce Stakes at Sandown on Lord Rosebery's Captain Kidd.

Sir Adrian Jarvis's Test Case (E. Larkin up) after winning the Gimcrack Stakes. Sir Adrian is standing next to me and Lord Rosebery just behind him. On my right is Roger Parris, for many years my head lad.

of the mud. What had been gritty dirt pulverised almost to a powder, was now slop. Beneath it was hard foundation. Piccadilly is not harder than the foundation of this track. Apparently there was no such thing as percolation. Here, then, an entirely new set of conditions and circumstances were presented. Some dolls were stretched across the track to prevent trainers working their horses. I had them down and gave Papyrus a canter round one of the turns.

Now, as to our opponent I may describe him as a dark brown horse, in fact of nearly the same colour as Papyrus. Some people may have thought it remarkable that two horses brought together in such circumstances and after so much negotiation and trouble should have been coloured exactly alike. After all there are so many chestnuts and bays in the horse world, many of them good horses too, to say nothing of the greys which have come into such prominence in recent years. Zev stood just on 16 hands, and perhaps the first thing one noticed about him is that he has an ugly head. He is also what we call rather 'on the leg', but he always gave me the impression, on the whole, of being a business-like sort, without, however, being particularly distinguished. His shoulders are a trifle heavy, and altogether he gives you the idea of being more of a sprinter than a stayer.

Somehow I lean to the idea that if it had not rained Zev would not have been America's chosen representative. At the last minute as it seemed they sent for Admiral Grayson's colt My Own, who, however, had a long and tedious journey from his training quarters through a breakdown in the transport. According to

113

the terms of the agreement with us he was to understudy Zev in the event of anything happening to that horse, and from the fact of his being sent for rather hurriedly one gained the idea that they were not altogether satisfied with the condition of Zev, who, after all, had been in hard training ever since last February. They may also have been frightened for the first time by the excellent showing of Papyrus in that gallop he did two days before the race and to which I have referred. However, the coming of the rain in such quantity settled the whole matter. Zev being what they call a great 'mudder', was deputed for duty.

The matter of the plating of Papyrus now arises. I have been much criticised for not plating the horse on the American method of having gripping tips and caulks introduced to the shoe. Perhaps I was wrong in not doing as they do in America, and in not accepting the well-meant advice of several of the American trainers. But I should like at this point to put the position as viewed by me. In the first place Papyrus had never worked such plates in his life. There is a danger from the wearing of such plates of the horse over-reaching himself and cutting himself so severely as to put himself right out of action. I had not the faintest notion how the colt would perform in them, whether in fact he would do himself an injury or whether he would even give of his proper action. My first objective was to get him to the post in the condition he was when I galloped him, and I could run no unnecessary risk.

All his work on the dry track had been done in his English plates and he strode out all right. He

114

gave that last good gallop in such plates and that was good enough for me. I knew his action was right, so, therefore, why experiment? But then came the rain to alter everything. Again, I was made to understand that to avoid slipping in slush I would be well advised to adopt the American shoes, but I was afraid that he might be unable to act in them. If anything happened by which he might be injured or fail to show his action I felt I would be blamed for adopting methods with which I was entirely unfamiliar. So, rightly or wrongly, I stuck to the English plates. I am sure in the light of the result that I was wrong. We should all profit by our experiences and doubtless were the race to be run again I would adopt the American methods of plating with the clips and caulks. It was a most difficult position in which I found myself— between the devil and the sea—but it was only after much thought and weighing of the chances that I decided to abide by the plates in which the horse had done so well forty-eight hours before. After all how was I to know that the track, once so dry and dusty, would be transformed into a condition which it is absolutely beyond me to describe.

My orders to Donoghue were to be with Zev all the way, to be on his outside and so avoid any risk of being shut in at the bends. I had seen interference of the sort happen on one or two of the courses I had visited, for it is quite true that in America the jockeys do not keep quite such a straight course as we do in England. Donoghue was then to trust his horse's speed and stamina to win his race in the short home stretch or run in.

As it happened Donoghue got the best of the start.

No doubt the starter, if anyone was to be favoured, was keen to let such an advantage be with the visiting horse. Anyhow there was Donoghue out clear by a couple of lengths, and I suppose if his orders had not been what they were he would have gone on and made the best of his advantage. However, he deliberately took a pull at his horse, thereby enabling Sande to rush Zev into the lead next to the rails. I first realised that Papyrus would not win after they had gone four furlongs. They were then travelling along the back stretch parallel to the straight for home and the grand stand. Papyrus, I could see was slipping and not gaining a proper foot-hold. He was showing fear too of extending himself, and the jockey confirmed this when he came back.

I could see our horse lose three quarters of a length every time he slipped, and then he would again draw up to Zev, but, of course, this could not go on. He was being rapidly exhausted, and when they came to make the last turn it was all up with him. As things were we were fairly licked. That was plain enough for all to see, but if I was wrong in the matter of the plating of my horse then I cannot accept Zev as being the better, allowing, also for the disadvantageous conditions under which Papyrus had laboured from the moment he left England. It was an absolute tragedy for us that the rain should have come when it did and how it did. On the dry ground the English plates, while they may not have been a help, would certainly not have been a hindrance as they proved to be in the sloppy going. Therefore, I do not hesitate to say that had the going remained dry Papyrus would most certainly have won.

He pulled up tired as one would expect him to do in the circumstances, but he was not unduly distressed, and afterwards he showed no ill effects of his race. I should add that Donoghue was pulling up his horse before the finish otherwise the margin would have been less than two lengths.

In my opinion we need never be afraid of America taking away our supremacy in breeding as some people might imagine would be the case as the result of this race. That is as long as they race on the lines which appear to be the fashion with them now. They will never be able to prove they have a great horse because of the way they break down their horses. They call their four-year-olds 'veterans', and so far as I could discover, there are few if any of them in training. They do not seem to have any horses of any account older than three years of age. A great many of the two-year-olds I saw are either blistered or fired.

It is not their dirt tracks I take exception to so much as the fact that their horses must be trained as well as raced on them. We have Epsom and Ascot frequently very hard, too hard in fact for ideal racing, but the point is that the horses performing there have probably been trained on good going and, therefore, they do not arrive there particularly broken down. Every racehorse in America seems to get a hard race because of the system they have of running their races. Jockeys jump off and ride most desperately right from what they call the 'break'. I suppose the tactics are necessary in order to secure a good place at the first turn. Anyhow while the times are good at the start they fall away at the finish which is different to the way our races are run. They do not do better times than we do in England.

I cannot close these notes without bearing my humble tribute to the sportsmanship shown by the Americans all through, and to the magnificent way they received us and tried to do everything possible for us. Nothing was too great a trouble for them if it could add to our welfare and that of the horse. The Jockey Club entertained us, and after the race Mr. Belmont as the head of the Jockey Club entertained us. One could not doubt the expressions of goodwill towards us in their sincerity. It was apparent on every hand wherever we went. I am positive that had Papyrus won the victory would have been better received than was actually the case with Zev. This may seem hard to understand at home. But it undoubtedly was so. The American trainers, too, to a man were splendid.

Surely it was a great moment when the American band on the course struck up 'God Save the King' and thirty or forty thousand Americans immediately stood up and uncovered to our King. Where else could that have happened? And in what other foreign country in the world? And we by our visit with Papyrus had done it. That surely was something for us to be proud of and to remember to the end of our days. Perhaps it was the most vivid and lasting impression of all. Then did the Aquitania's band return the compliment by playing the Star Spangled Banner. So I say that we did not go in vain even though we were beaten, and to say that we have discredited the British thoroughbred and done all this for sordid gain is a lie. We have helped along the better feeling

118

and understanding between the two great nations, and though you, who were not there, may not think so, yet it is an outstanding and shining fact of which I shall ever be proud.

As I close these notes I have before me a letter received just before sailing from a notable English journalist in New York. He has twenty years experience of New York and America, and he writes—'Quite apart from the sporting side the cause of friendship has been helped quite a lot by the splendid impression created by the friends of Papyrus visiting this side. It is my opinion, speaking from twenty years experience of this city, that you have done more good than many newspaper despatches in cementing the entente which is yet destined to secure the peace, and I hope prosperity of our troubled world.'

CHAPTER X

During World War II a staff of old men and boys enabled me to keep the stable going. In a way it was rather unfortunate that in this period I happened to have a lot of really good horses as of course prize money was scarce and opportunities few. During the years that Lord Rosebery and I owned the Sandwich Stud together, we had at least one runner placed in a classic every season.

A rattling good horse that came to me as a yearling in 1943 was Sir John Jarvis's Royal Charger, a handsome, powerful chestnut colt by Nearco out of Sun Princess, a Solario mare whose grandam was the famous 'Flying Filly', Mumtaz Mahal. Nearco won the Grand Prix and Solario the St. Leger and the Gold Cup so no doubt it was from Mumtaz Mahal that Royal Charger inherited his speed.

In his early days Royal Charger showed little sign of living up to his looks and his pedigree and, but for obstinacy on my part that really amounted to pig-headedness, he would probably have been sold out of the stable for a few hundred pounds. In the end Sir John was able to sell him for something like £80,000.

Much to my disappointment Royal Charger went badly when I galloped him, and when I galloped him a second time he went no better. I thought he might show up a bit better in a race but he performed without distinction and Eph Smith, who rode him, said he was no good. Accordingly I advised Sir John to put him in the sales and this was done.

At the back of my mind, though, I still had a strong feeling that Royal Charger was basically a good horse, so I decided to give him another run. I instructed Eph to wake him up but Eph omitted to do so on the grounds that it was pointless hitting a bad horse. His humanitarian instincts did him credit but it would have been better if he had obeyed my orders. At the following Newmarket meeting Royal Charger was in a race that I confidently expected to win with Lord Milford's Sun Honey, who would be ridden by Eph. I asked Sir John if I could engage Bobby Jones, a very strong rider, for Royal Charger and Sir John gave his consent. Royal Charger was well behind early on but when Bobby gave him 'one for the road' he fairly flew and in the end he finished only a length and a half behind Sun Honey who won. Royal Charger was withdrawn from the sale forthwith.

The following season Royal Charger won three races, including the Challenge Stakes, and was third to two very good horses, Court Martial and Dante, in the Two Thousand Guineas. At four he was better still, winning the Queen Anne Stakes at Royal Ascot and in the autumn the Ayr Gold Cup with 9st. 7, a magnificent performance. As I said earlier, Sir John sold him to the Irish National Stud for round about £80,000, and the Irish National Stud re-sold him to

America for some £200,000 when the Stud purchased Tulyar. Royal Charger sired Happy Laughter (One Thousand Guineas), Gilles de Retz (Two Thousand Guineas) and Sea Charger (Irish Two Thousand and Irish St. Leger). In America he got Turn To, the best two-year-old in the United States in 1954 and grandsire of the 1968 Derby winner, Sir Ivor.

In 1944 I won my second Derby for Lord Rosebery, the horse in question being Ocean Swell, one of Blue Peter's first crop of runners, out of Jiffy, by Hurry On. Training such a wonderful horse as Blue Peter had perhaps rather spoilt me as afterwards I was inclined to judge other good horses by Blue Peter's exceptional standard and of course they never measured up to it. Ocean Swell was clearly not such a good horse as his sire but he was a fine stayer with any amount of courage.

In appearance Ocean Swell was a workmanlike bay. He never carried much flesh when he was hard-trained and in his early days he was inclined to be leggy. He was rather slow to come to hand and was unplaced in his first three ventures, but in the autumn he showed marked improvement by finishing second in the Isleham Plate and he then displayed encouraging speed by winning the six furlong Alington Plate, also at Newmarket, from nineteen opponents, among whom were that fine sprinter Golden Cloud and Tehran, the latter destined to win the St. Leger. I well remember that after the Alington Plate my friend Meyrick Good, who wrote for so many years for the *Sporting Life*, came up to me and observed with no little emphasis: 'That horse, Jack, will win the Derby.'

Ocean Swell came on a bit during the winter and he started off well enough by winning the ten furlong Column Stakes at Newmarket. On May 3rd, though, he could only finish third over the same distance to Borealis. In the Two Thousand Guineas a fortnight later Eph Smith rode Honeyway for me and Billy Nevett rode Ocean Swell, who started at 33/1. The distance was all too short for Ocean Swell who finished well down the course, the race being won by Lord Derby's filly Garden Path by inches from Growing Confidence with Tehran third. Billy Nevett said there was no excuse to be made and the horse was just not good enough.

Honeyway did not run in the Derby and Eph begged off Ocean Swell as he had a chance of riding Growing Confidence in the big race. Lord Rosebery agreed to this and Billy Nevett was engaged for Ocean Swell. It so happened that Eph's arrangement to ride Growing Confidence fell through, but of course our arrangement with Nevett held good. In the end Eph got the ride on Tehran, Gordon Richards having been claimed to ride the Beckhampton representative, Mustang.

The Derby proved to be a thrilling race. Ocean Swell's stamina and courage just gained him the day and he held on to win by a neck from Tehran with Happy Landing a short head away third. The fly in the ointment was that Lord Rosebery was unable to leave his duties in Scotland, while my wife and I were both unwell and in bed at home. We listened-in to the race and I had a nice bet on Ocean Swell just before the 'Off'. His starting price was the remunerative one of 28/1. That evening Lady Rosebery and

123

her step-daughter, Lady Helen Smith, came up to our bedroom and told us the details of Ocean Swell's triumph.

Ocean Swell did not run again before the St. Leger. Unfortunately about a month before the race his lead horse hurt himself and I had not got a suitable horse to work with Ocean Swell. He ran a very honest race but found a couple too good for him in Tehran and Borealis, the latter a half-brother to that great stayer Alycidon. Ocean Swell finished the season in fine style by winning the two and a quarter mile Jockey Club Cup by three lengths from the five-year-old Historic. As a result of that victory, Lord Rosebery decided to keep him in training for another year with the Gold Cup as his main objective.

Ocean Swell began his final season by beating his old rival Borealis in the April Stakes at Newmarket, but Borealis then beat him both in the Wood Ditton Stakes and the Coronation Cup. The memory of these defeats, though, was wiped out by Ocean Swell's victory in the Gold Cup, run at Ascot for the first time since 1939. In achieving this success Ocean Swell was the first Derby winner to win a Gold Cup run at Ascot since Persimmon in 1897. Although totally unsuited to the firm ground, Tehran was a hot favourite at 7/4 on. Borealis started at 5/1 while Ocean Swell, who did not carry an ounce of superfluous flesh, was on offer at 6/1. Tehran was going smoothly in the lead round the final bend but in the straight Eph Smith brought Ocean Swell with one long run and in the final furlong he showed by far the better speed to beat Tehran by a length and a half with Abbots Fell third. This was my fourth

Gold Cup success and it was Ocean Swell's last race. Unfortunately he proved disappointing as a sire and his stock were liable to inherit his less attractive physical characteristics without his admirable racing ability.

Just about the gamest filly I ever trained was Lord Rosebery's Ribbon. By Fairway out of that good staying mare Bongrace, she was very small but her courage made up for her lack of inches. As a two-year-old she was beaten first time out but won her next four races. In the Middle Park Stakes she took on the colts and won, beating the Aga Khan's Nasrullah after a terrific battle. That race undoubtedly left its mark on Nasrullah; he remembered it next year and it was not easy to get him to go down to the post.

Ribbon did grow a little during the winter but in 1943 she was still very small, her lack of size being if anything emphasised by her neat, compact appearance. She was perfectly proportioned and a filly of lovely quality. Her first race as a three-year-old was the Upwell Stakes at Newmarket on May 4th. The distance was all too short for her but she fought on with her usual courage and won by a short head from Open Warfare with Lord Derby's Herringbone third. In the One Thousand Guineas run at the end of May, Ribbon again ran a game race but she found one just too good for her in Herringbone who beat her on her merits by a neck.

Ribbon was desperately unlucky not to win the Oaks. As the tapes went up Noontide swerved right in front of Ribbon who was just beginning to move forward. Ribbon had to turn to avoid a collision. She not only lost lengths, but was left facing the wrong way, thereby forfeiting all her normal and natural impulse. I did not think she stood a chance after that, but she gradually made up ground and in the final furlong she drew up to the leader, Mr. J. V. Rank's Why Hurry, and put in a tremendous challenge. It was a wonderful race between two very game fillies but Why Hurry just held on to win by a neck.

Time is a great healer, so they say, but I still feel sore about the St. Leger. Poor little Ribbon had a terribly rough passage and was bumped and knocked all over the place. She would not be denied, though, and putting her head down she battled on like the little heroine she was. I have no doubt in my own mind that she won by a neck and as far as I could make out everyone else on the course thought so too. There was one exception, though, and that was the Judge, Major Petch. His verdict was that Herringbone had won by a short head. Whenever I look at a photograph of the finish of that race, I am convinced that my opinion is correct and that Ribbon was 'robbed'.

There is no doubt that the fillies were pretty good that year and among the colts behind Herringbone and Ribbon in the St. Leger were the Derby winner Straight Deal, Nasrullah, Persian Gulf, Kingsway, and Umiddad.

Lord Rosebery was very keen to end Ribbon's racing career with a win and accordingly it was decided to run her in the Jockey Club Cup in October. Bad luck, though, dogged her to the end. At that time there were a lot of American Air Force stores parked on the Heath by the Cambridge Road, including a lot of barbed wire. Walking down to the July course, Ribbon was scared by a patrolling jeep. She whipped round, reared up and fell on her right side. She then picked herself up and galloped off into the town where she was caught. Her stifle was cut and she was grazed, but as she seemed perfectly sound we allowed her to take her chance. It was noticeable, though, that as she went down to the post she moved her near hind leg stiffly and no doubt her injuries were causing her to stiffen up. It was then too late to withdraw her. She never showed her true form and sad to say finished unplaced behind Mr. Allnutt's Shahpoor.

Another good, game filly of Lord Rosebery's was Afterthought, by Obliterate out of the One Thousand Guineas winner Plack. Foaled in 1939, she was Plack's first foal since 1933. As a three-year-old Afterthought was fourth in the One Thousand Guineas, second to the brilliant Sun Chariot in the Oaks, second in the Gold Cup and second in the Champion Stakes, too. She won a wonderful race for the Jockey Club Cup by a head and a short head from High Table and Bakhtawar. Her dam had won that same race too. At the stud she bred four winners and was grandam of Beta, a very nice filly that won the Royal Lodge Stakes at Ascot.

Two good Hyperion colts that ran for Lord Rosebery in the war were Hippius and Hyperides. Hippius, a little black colt, won the Champion Stakes twice, on the first occasion beating the Derby winner Pont L'Evêque. He was also third to Turkhan in the war-substitute St. Leger. Hyperides was second in the 1942 Derby and the following season won the Coronation Cup. In the Derby he was in front fifty yards from the post but was then headed by Watling Street who ran on to beat him by a neck. Both Hippius and Hyperides died young. Sold for 3,000 guineas to go to Brazil, Hippius died at sea in 1941 in appalling weather. Hyperides was sold to Lady Yule as a stallion but died a year or two later.

Quite one of the best horses I trained that never won a classic was Lord Milford's Honeyway, a grand stamp of brown horse by Fairway out of that great brood mare Honey Buzzard, a half-sister by Papyrus to Flamingo. Honeyway made his reputation as a sprinter but before he retired he had shown that he possessed stamina as well by winning the Champion Stakes of a mile and a quarter. Furthermore he won over a mile and a half at Thirsk during his final season's racing. Other victories included the Victoria Cup with top weight, the Cork and Orrery Stakes at Ascot, the July Cup and the King George Stakes at Goodwood.

At the close of his five-year-old season Honeyway was syndicated at a capitalised value of £72,000. The snag, though, lay in the fact that he was a double rig. Lord Milford, therefore, agreed in the contract to re-purchase any share in the syndicate from the original purchaser for £1,200 on or before June 30th 1948 if asked to do so. After covering a few mares Honeyway was tested and found to be sterile so back he came to me to be trained again and I won three more races with him. At the end of that season he went back again to stud but his testicles had not yet descended and again his fertility proved a source of anxiety. He was accordingly withdrawn from his duties and was treated, coming back cured in 1949.

128

Above: On the boat to South Africa. Three Jacks (in the centre of the picture) Jack Jarvis, Jack Hobbs and Jack Solomons. *Left:* My godson William Jarvis, Ryan Jarvis's son, leads in his Aunt Sally Hall, after winning the Newmarket Town Plate in 1965.

Above: Lord Howard de Walden presents me with a cigar-box at Ayr. *Below:* Off to Buckingham Palace to receive my Knighthood. My daughter Vivien is on my right. On my left is my secretary, Mrs. Smallwood.

In 1953 he had a fertility percentage of 91.18. Once he got going, he proved a very good sire. Among his best winners were Dictaway (French One Thousand), Honeylight (One Thousand Guineas) and Great Nephew, who only lost the Two Thousand by a matter of inches.

CHAPTER XI

With the end of the war, racing began to get going again. To old-timers like myself it was very reminiscent of the aftermath of the Kaiser's war. There was a terrific racing boom and the attendances were enormous. The betting was on a lavish scale, too, and many young men seemed determined to get rid of their gratuities with the utmost speed, a procedure in which they received the maximum co-operation from the bookmakers. Fortunes had been made in industry in the war, and on the black market, too, and there was an influx of new owners, some of whom did not bring any noticeable benefit to the sport. Most of the less desirable ones did not last very long. The pace, however, had been pretty hot while it lasted.

In 1945 I had a very nice Hyperion three-year-old belonging to Lord Rosebery called Midas. He won the Newmarket Stakes, then an important Derby trial, by four lengths and in the Derby itself he ran a fine race to finish second to Dante. Unfortunately he developed 'a leg' afterwards and never ran again. Lord Rosebery sold him privately to Mr. J. A. C. Lilley and this was my first meeting with my friend

Claude Lilley for whom I subsequently trained a number of good horses including Pretendre, who so nearly won the Derby in 1966. Midas was not a success as a sire and was exported to America in 1956. My best three-year-old filly in 1945 was Lord Rosebery's Blue Smoke, a Blue Peter filly that was second to Sun Stream in the One Thousand Guineas. The following year Lord Rosebery had another very nice filly in Iona who was third in the One Thousand Guineas and second in the Oaks. She won the Wood Ditton Stakes and the Lingfield Oaks Trial. Being a half-sister to Ocean Swell by Hyperion, she had immense stud potentialities but did not do as well as we hoped, although one of her daughters, Skye, won over £5,000 in stakes.

In 1951 I was second in the Derby with Lord Milford's Sybil's Nephew, the best horse sired by Midas. He was officially described as by Honeyway or Midas but there is little doubt that in fact he was by Midas. The winner of the Derby that year was Arctic Prince who won most decisively by six lengths. There is no doubt that he was a really good horse and it was a pity he broke down in the King George VI and Queen Elizabeth Stakes. Sybil's Nephew, who had won over the Rowley Mile as a two-year-old, was a true stayer and I very much expected him to win the St. Leger for which he started favourite at 13/2. He ran disappointingly, however, and finished down the course.

That St. Leger was a most extraordinary race. In the paddock M. M. Boussac's Talma II put up a deplorable exhibition. Sweating profusely, he was in a most excitable condition and without going into details his behaviour was more like that of a stallion than a three-year-old about to participate in a classic. Normally such conduct causes a horse to recede in the betting but Talma started at 7/1 and was undoubtedly the best backed horse on the day.

The confidence of Talma's supporters was fully justified by the result of the race as he swept into the lead three quarters of a mile from home and drew clear to win with astonishing ease by a margin which the judge estimated as ten lengths but which to many of those present looked nearer twenty. Never before that race or after it did Talma show comparable form. I was all the more mystified when in the two mile Cumberland Lodge Stakes at Ascot the following month Talma, conceding only 3lbs. was flat out to beat Eastern Emperor, whom I trained for Lord Milford, by a neck. I still sometimes ponder over the secret of Talma's spreadeagling victory at Doncaster.

Sybil's Nephew won the Hastings Stakes, Dee Stakes and Newmarket St. Leger as a three-year-old. The following season he won the Manchester Cup with 9 stone and was second in the Coronation Cup and the Doncaster Cup. He really ought to have won the Doncaster Cup but Bill Rickaby did not ride one of his brainiest races. Instead of waiting and pouncing on the temperamental Aquino II, who was quite liable to run out if left in front, he chose to take him on a long way from home and got the worst of it. Sybil's Nephew was exported to South Africa and was doing very well as a sire when unfortunately he died young.

I was very fond of Eastern Emperor, a black colt by Hyperion out of a mare by Tiberius. He was tough and game and raced until he was six. He won five races as a three-year-old, including the Jockey Club Cup. As a four-year-old he was a really good stayer. He started off by finishing second in the Chester Cup, giving 8lbs. to the winner, Le Tellier. He then won the Yorkshire Cup and he would very likely have won the Winston Churchill Stakes at Hurst Park if he had not been baulked when making his challenge. I thought he might win me my fifth Gold Cup but his challenge was delayed by interference from tiring horses in front of him and when he got clear the French-bred Aquino II, trained by Sam Armstrong, had a lead of two lengths. Eastern Emperor tackled him in great style and narrowed the gap but with Gordon Richards riding his hardest, Aquino held on to win by less than a length. In a slow-run race for the Goodwood Cup—the time was 33 seconds slower than the record set up by Fearless Fox—Eastern Emperor was second to Medway. The following season he won the Chester Cup carrying 9st. 2 and the Winston Churchill Stakes but then he rather lost his form and was unplaced in the Gold Cup behind Souepi on whom Elliott rode a superlative race.

In 1953 I won the One Thousand Guineas with Mr. David Wills's Happy Laughter, a very good filly whose career was a constant battle against ill-health. Bred at the Ballykisteen Stud, Happy Laughter was a very attractive chestnut filly by Royal Charger, whom I had trained, out of Bray Melody. Acting on Mr. Wills's behalf, I bought her for 3,500 guineas at the Doncaster Sales. As a two-year-old she did very well and won five races including the Stud Produce Stakes at Sandown and the Acorn Stakes at Epsom.

Her successes were all the more noteworthy as she was never really right. She sweated up a lot and suffered continually from sinus trouble. It was probably catarrhal infection that was responsible for her defeat in the Lowther Stakes at York. In the Free Handicap she was rated 12lbs. below the other good two-year-old filly I had that season, Sir Adrian Jarvis's Tessa Gillian, a full-sister to Royal Charger.

At the end of the season Happy Laughter was sent to her owner's stud and it was hoped that nature might effect a cure where veterinary science had so far failed. However Colonel Douglas Gray, Mr. Wills's manager, reported after a time that not only was Happy Laughter not improving but she had developed a big lump under her eye. She failed to respond to sulphonamide treatment so Mr. Wills sought the advice of a Harley Street nose and throat specialist who advocated surgical treatment. Accordingly an operation was performed at the Equine Research Station at Newmarket. The orbital bone was trephined and the right maxillary sinus drained. She must have been suffering a lot as when the incision was made a mass of pus shot out.

It was found that Happy Laughter was suffering from three different infections. Two were rapidly dealt with but for the third aureomycin was necessary and at that time aureomycin was virtually unobtainable in England. Colonel Gray was therefore sent to see the appropriate Government officials in Ireland. Ireland is a nation of horselovers and furthermore Happy Laughter's sire Royal Charger was then standing at the Irish National Stud; a supply of the drug was forthcoming.

Clearly Happy Laughter was going to have a restricted preparation for the One Thousand Guineas and when she did rejoin my stable at the beginning of February she still had a hole in her head that needed dressing night and morning. At that stage I obviously could do very little with her and it was only a month before the One Thousand that I gave her her first sharp canter.

I decided that the best thing for Happy Laughter would be to give her a race at the Craven Meeting and so I ran her in the Free Handicap. Of course she was still very backward and furthermore she was badly away but she delighted me by running a wonderful race under the circumstances, finishing second to Good Brandy who was receiving 5lbs.

In the One Thousand Guineas Tessa Gillian was ridden by Bill Rickaby, the stable jockey, and Manny Mercer was up on Happy Laughter. A small but beautifully proportioned bay filly, Tessa Gillian had thrown a splint as a two-year-old and had been unable to run before the Molecomb Stakes at Goodwood, which she won. She then won the Prince of Wales's Stakes at York and two other races but in the Cheveley Park Stakes she went under by a matter of inches to Mr. J. S. Gerber's Bebe Grande. Tessa Gillian had begun her three-year-old career in style by beating a strong field for the Katheryn Howard Stakes at Hurst Park. In the One Thousand Guineas she started at 9/2, half a point longer than Bebe Grande. Happy Laughter was easy to back at 10/1. The closing stages of the race concerned only those three. Bebe Grande began to falter on the hill and perhaps was feeling the effect of her hard race two days previously in the Two Thousand Guineas in which she was second to Nearula. Happy Laughter mastered Tessa Gillian and ran on gallantly to win by two lengths, thereby giving Manny Mercer his first classic success. She did not quite stay the distance in the Oaks, in which she was fourth, but she showed what a magnificent filly she was up to ten furlongs by winning all her last three races, the Coronation Stakes at Ascot, the Falmouth Stakes at Newmarket and the Nassau Stakes at Goodwood.

With a bit of luck I might have won the Two Thousand Guineas and the Derby in 1966 as I had three very good colts in Great Nephew, General Gordon and Pretendre. However, things did not go quite my way.

Great Nephew was bred and owned by Mr. Jim Philipps, son of my old patron Lord Milford, and is by that grand horse Honeyway out of Sybil's Niece by Admiral's Walk, all three of whom I had trained. I decided to give Great Nephew a race at the Kempton Easter Meeting and he was going so well in it that unfortunately it was difficult to restrain him and he struck into another horse on the final bend and came down. The Epsom trainer 'Boggy' Whelan who was watching the race at that point assured me afterwards that Great Nephew had the race at his mercy when disaster overtook him. It did not help matters that Great Nephew cut himself and his preparation was in consequence interrupted, while furthermore his fall had deprived him of the full benefit of a race. In the Two Thousand Guineas, ridden by Bill Rickaby and starting at 66/1, he was beaten a short head by Kashmir II. Needless to say I was rather disappointed when later in the season Mr. Philipps sent Great Nephew to be trained by Pollet in France.

General Gordon was a chestnut colt by Never Say Die that belonged to Lord Rosebery. As a two-year-old he split a pastern and never saw a racecourse. The following season he started off by finishing third in the Wood Ditton Stakes at Newmarket. This brought him on nicely and he really began to improve. He won the Chester Vase impressively and at that point he seemed to have a great career ahead of him, but in his final Derby gallop he broke a leg and had to be destroyed. Brian Taylor, who rode him, said he was pulling over the other horses in the gallop including Pretendre, who only lost the Derby by a neck. Lord Rosebery accepted this cruel blow like the good sportsman that he is. He had a bit of ill-luck two years previously when Fighting Ship, a very good stayer by Doutelle and a likely winner of the Ascot Gold Cup, broke down when winning the Henry II Stakes at Sandown.

Pretendre, a big chestnut colt by Doutelle, was bred by H.R.H. the Princess Royal and Mr. Claude Lilley bought him as a foal for 3,600 guineas at the December Sales. Pretendre took a longish time to come to hand and it was not until the autumn that he really showed signs of being of classic calibre. At Sandown in September he pleased me a lot when he ran second over a mile to Lord Rosebery's useful St. Puckle, who was receiving 12lbs. He then won in succession the seven furlong Dewhurst Stakes at Newmarket and the one mile Observer Gold Cup at Doncaster. The latter race was worth over £21,000 to the winner and is the most valuable prize I have ever won. At the end of the season Pretendre was given 9st. 10 in the Free Handicap and was rated inferior only to Prendergast's speedy Young Emperor.

Pretendre grew the right way during the winter and he worked impressively in the spring. His first outing was in the Blue Riband Trial Stakes at Epsom and the brilliant manner in which he won that event brought back memories of Blue Peter. After that victory Mr. Lilley and I decided to let him take his chance in the Two Thousand Guineas, but he ran far less well than I had anticipated, finishing eighth, a long way behind Kashmir II and my other runner, Great Nephew. It was a very fast-run race and I think Pretendre was really carried off his legs in the early stages. Moreover he was a stayer rather than a miler.

Pretendre started joint favourite for the Derby with a big, plain Irish colt, Right Noble, and he ran a magnificent race. After saddling him I got held up returning to the grandstand and in fact I never got on the stand at all and watched the contest from ground level. I was a bit worried when the commentator failed to mention Pretendre early on and my colt was still some way behind the leaders at Tattenham Corner. From three furlongs out, though, he began to make up ground fast and when he led by a neck with just over a furlong to go I really thought he was going to win. Charlottown, however, put in a terrific challenge. This took him half a length in front of Pretendre, who refused to give in, though, and was only a neck behind Charlottown at the winning post. Young Paul Cook rode Pretendre beautifully through the race but I rather wish he had used his whip in the final hundred yards. I never relish seeing a game horse hit, but a single sharp reminder might conceivably have done the trick, and after all, the Derby is the Derby. Scobie Breasley on Charlottown had wonderful luck as he came through on the rails the whole way, tactics that would have landed him in trouble nineteen years out of twenty.

Pretendre won the King Edward VII Stakes at Ascot but was unplaced in the St. Leger. Before the Leger a well-known bloodstock agency had bought him for a client in America, but after Doncaster the client seemed far from keen to complete the transaction. Pretendre remained in my stable for a long time and it was worrying looking after this horse worth over £150,000 and not really knowing who owned him. Mr Lilley was sympathetic—he of course was worried, too—and did all that he could to help. The climax came when a man from the agency turned up unheralded to collect Pretendre at midnight without either a letter of authority or proof of identity. The whole incident annoyed me considerably and when I next met the member of the agency who had conducted the transaction, I told him some things that I think rather surprised him. I hope they did, anyway.

CHAPTER XII

Now that I am over eighty I have two ambitions left in racing—to win the Oaks, the one classic that has so far eluded me, and to complete my two thousandth winner. I hope during the coming season I shall be assisted in achieving at least one of these objectives by young John Gorton who is coming from South Africa to ride for me.

I have not the slightest intention of indulging in political controversy and I am well aware that South Africa usually gets a bad press nowadays, particularly from people who have never been there, but I freely admit that I love South Africa, that I have always been happy there, and that I have many South African friends. I first went to South Africa on a combined business and pleasure trip in 1936, and bar the war years, I have been there almost every winter since. I find that my holiday there just about sets me up for the year. I always travel out there by sea and among the valued friends I made on the voyage was that superlative cricketer and most modest and likeable personality, Sir Jack Hobbs.

One of my best South African friends is Jack Stubbs who runs a most successful stud at Capetown. He had a stallion there called Dialogue, by Hyperion, and as Hyperion blood blends well with Blue Peter blood, I suggested to him that he ought to have a mare by Blue Peter. He acquired Pam, a three-year-old filly by Blue Peter, and I am happy to say she has been a great success.

I celebrated my eightieth birthday in South Africa. I gave a big party at which my friends presented me with a painting of Table Mountain as seen from the Blue Peter Restaurant. During the party I showed them a film of the highlight of my racing career, Blue Peter's Derby victory.

Life for a trainer with a big stable of valuable horses is an arduous and responsible one, particularly in recent years when shortage of labour during the winter has always been a worry. I have had two great advantages that have helped to keep me going over the years; first, a wonderfully happy home life in which, since my wife died, my daughter Vivien has been a marvellous and utterly unselfish companion to me. Secondly, I have had the benefit of a loyal and competent staff. Earlier on I mentioned Percy Double who came to me as Head Lad when I started and remained with me, except during World War I, till he died. Percy shared my interests in, and love for, racing pigeons. In the Kaiser's war, when methods of military communication were rather less sophisticated than they are today, I was attached as a signals N.C.O. to the Tanks Corps, it being deemed expedient at the time for every tank to be equipped with a couple of pigeons for delivering messages. At the end of the war I was an instructor at Bovingdon and was lecturing young officers about the handling of pigeons on the morning of November 11th, 1918. During my discourse an officer poked his head round the door and shouted 'The war's over!' Whereupon, without a second's hesitation, my class headed for the door and left me standing there. I can't say I blame them.

Another employee to whom I feel greatly indebted is Charlie Lake, for many years my second Head Lad, while Roger Parris, my Travelling Head Lad, has been with me for over forty years. Roger came to me as an apprentice and lodged with Percy Double, who formed a high opinion of him. When I first appointed him, Roger must have been the youngest Travelling Head Lad at Newmarket. I have never regretted my choice.

In recent years I have come to be grateful in running the stable for the help I have had from my old friend Bobby Jones, who was of course in his younger days a top-class jockey. I am indebted, too, to Cyril Gibson, who came here as an apprentice, then rode for many years in Cairo and Alexandria, and eventually returned to Park Lodge. David Leader, who acted as my assistant trainer, was, alas, killed in the war. For some years after it, Harry Jelliss occupied that position.

When I was younger I always tried to take a useful and constructive part in local affairs as I thought it essential that the interests of the racing community should be explained to the various local authorities. When I was a member of the County Council I was instrumental in thwarting a move to do away with the Fire Station at Newmarket, which would have resulted in reliance on the Fire Services at Bury St.

Edmunds. Because of the ever-present danger of fire in racing stables, that would have meant taking an unwarrantable risk.

I also took great interest in the establishment of Exning House as an Old People's Home. When I approached Mr. G. C. Gibson with a view to buying Exning House for that purpose, Mr. Gibson, with wonderful generosity, presented Exning House free, with no strings attached, and furthermore presented £10,000 for furtherance of the scheme. The only stipulation he made was that it should be known as Glanely House after his uncle, Lord Glanely, who had formerly lived there. I was also Chairman of a successful Appeals Committee at Newmarket that raised a considerable sum of money for Addenbrooke's Hospital, Cambridge.

Of my interests outside racing I have already mentioned coursing and my Waterloo Cup victory with Jovial Judge. Much as I loved coursing I had to give it up in World War II when, once rationing was introduced, feeding the dogs adequately became an insuperable problem. I am very fond of bowls, one of the few games left that is essentially for amateurs, and I was once invited to take a team to South Africa but unfortunately I had to refuse.

I love watching cricket and have passed many a happy hour at Fenners watching Cambridge. I think I am a fair judge of cricket form and after seeing a couple of innings by Ted Dexter, I ventured to tell the Duke of Norfolk that in Dexter Sussex was going to have the most polished and accomplished batsman since K. S. Duleepsinjhi. I used to ring up Fenners and if Dexter was batting or likely to go in soon, I

143

hurried over there as swiftly as I could.

I have always been passionately fond of shooting and I think I can claim to be a fairly adequate shot still. This autumn, shooting partridges with the Jockey Club, I managed to get a right and left. Not bad for over eighty! I love Scotland and have always enjoyed shooting grouse every August at the kind invitation of Lord Rosebery. Scotland has been good to me, too, as regards racing and in 1965 I was very touched to be presented with a silver cigar box there by Lord Howard de Walden on behalf of the Ayr executive. It was exactly sixty years since I had won the Ayr Gold Cup on Kilglass, owned by Lord Howard de Walden's father. I had hoped to record my hundreth winner at Ayr at that meeting but two of my fancied runners were defeated by horses trained by that large and genial Yorkshireman, Sam Hall. In my reply to the presentation, I mentioned that I had hoped to complete my century, but had unfortunately fallen under the substantial shadow of Sam Hall! The following year Dunlin and Creosote gave me my hundred winners at Ayr and that night I had a bit of a celebration with Mr. Tom Blackwell and Sir Alexander Sim, Chairman of the Horserace Totalisator Board.

One day many years ago I was walking back from a coursing meeting with Monty Collis-Browne and Mr. Jimmy Westoll, and Monty was ragging me about my allegedly inveterate good fortune in whatever I did. I mentioned that one thing I had never done—or even attempted to do—but very much wished to accomplish was to catch a salmon. Mr. Westoll thereupon said that if I really wanted to catch one, I ought to come up to his place in Cumberland at the start of the season. In due course Monty and I arrived at 6 a.m. on Carlisle Station and were met by Mr. Westoll, who captured my admiration by smoking a large and powerful pipe at that unfriendly hour of the morning. When we reached the river I had a few minutes' instruction and then, after one false start, made my first cast. I at once hooked a salmon which was duly landed despite the inconvenience of Monty jumping around and declaiming how indecently lucky I always was.

I have always loved a good party and one I always look forward to is the annual Dinner-Dance of the Twelve Club on the eve of the Derby. Membership of the Club, founded by Mr. Billy Long, is limited to a hundred, good sportsmen all. I became a member in 1929 and eventually succeeded Brigadier B. C. Hartley as President. It is quite an exhausting job conducting the auction after the draw for the Derby selling sweepstake but over the years I have derived a good deal of fun out of it.

Finally I should like to end on a very personal note and say how proud and honoured I was to be the recipient of a knighthood in 1967. The intimation of this came as a complete surprise to me and when a letter arrived giving me the news I was utterly taken aback. I just handed the letter to Vivien remarking 'Well, this is one for the books!'

I really felt it was an honour, not just for me, but for the little world of racing that has been my life. I went up to Buckingham Palace to receive my knighthood and as I knelt before the Queen I noted that the music played by the band in the background

145

was 'Puppet on a String'. I hope this had no significance. After the ceremony I motored back to Newmarket where I won a couple of races and the Queen won one, too. It was a great day for me and that evening I felt I had come quite a long way since I rode Black Friar for my father in a race for apprentices well over sixty years ago. I only wish my wife had been with me to share my happiness. By and large, though, I have been wonderfully lucky in most respects, as Monty Collis-Browne was so fond of pointing out, and I am truly grateful for a life that has brought me some success, much happiness and many good friends.

APPENDIX

Important Races Won

147

Queen Mary Stakes
  1951 Primavera
  1953 Sybils Niece

Queen's Vase (formerly
    Gold Vase)
  1922 Golden Myth
  1937 Fearless Fox
  1954 Prescription

Ribblesdale Stakes
  1953 Skye

Royal Lodge Stakes (run
    that year at Newbury)
  1960 Beta

St. James's Palace Stakes
  1923 Ellangowan
  1934 Flamenco
  1939 Admiral's Walk

Wokingham Stakes
  1920 Golden Orb
  1935 Theio

AYR
Ayr Gold Cup
  1937 Daytona
  1938 Old Reliance
  1946 Royal Charger

CHESTER
Chester Cup
  1953 Eastern Emperor
  1955 Prescription

Chester Vase
  1931 Sandwich
  1950 Castle Rock

  1952 Summer Rain
  1953 Empire Honey
  1962 Silver Cloud
  1966 General Gordon

DONCASTER
Doncaster Cup
  1922 Devizes
  1926 Bongrace
  1932 Foxhunter

Observer Gold Cup
  1965 Pretendre

Portland Handicap
  1924 Heverswood

EPSOM
Blue Riband Trial Stakes
  1939 Blue Peter
  1966 Pretendre

Coronation Cup (run at
    Newmarket on account
    of the war)
  1943 Hyperides

Great Metropolitan
  1949 Yoyo

Princess Elizabeth Stakes
  1951 Staffa

GOODWOOD
Chesterfield Cup
  1957 Rowland Ward

Goodwood Cup
  1933 Sans Peine
  1937 Fearless Fox

148

Goodwood Stakes
1946 Reynard Volant

Richmond Stakes
1963 Gentle Art

Stewards Cup
1963 Creole
1965 Potier

HURST PARK
Victoria Cup
1938 Phakos
1946 Honeyway
1951 Fastnet Rock
1961 Bass Rock

KEMPTON PARK
Great Jubilee Handicap
1950 Peter Flower

Queen's Prize
1922 Golden Myth
1933 Foxhunter
1951 Father Thames

LINCOLN
Lincolnshire Handicap
1935 Flamenco
1938 Phakos
1949 Fair Judgement

MANCHESTER
Manchester November Handicap
1934 Pip Emma
1939 Tutor
1952 Summer Rain

NEWBURY
Greenham Stakes
1963 Fighting Ship

NEWCASTLE
Northumberland Plate
1934 Whiteplains

NEWMARKET
Cambridgeshire
1954 Minstrel

Champion Stakes
1923 Ellangowan
1940 Hippius
1941 Hippius
1946 Honeyway
1950 Peter Flower

Cheveley Park Stakes
1957 Rich and Rare

Dewhurst Stakes
1965 Pretendre

Jockey Club Cup
1924 Plack
1926 Bongrace
1942 Afterthought
1944 Ocean Swell
1951 Eastern Emperor
1956 Donald

Jockey Club Stakes
1938 Challenge
1952 Master Cube
1964 Fighting Ship

July Cup
1945 Honeyway

149

July Stakes
- 1935 Daytona
- 1951 Bob Major
- 1952 Empire Honey
- 1963 Endless Honey

Middle Park Stakes
- 1942 Ribbon

Princess of Wales's Stakes
- 1962 Silver Cloud

- 1932 Miracle
- 1939 Blue Peter

National Stakes (formerly *National Breeders' Produce Stakes*)
- 1926 Priscilla
- 1927 Flamingo
- 1936 Full Sail
- 1953 Tudor Honey
- 1958 Captain Kidd

REDCAR
William Hill Gold Cup
- 1963 Campaign

SANDOWN PARK
Eclipse Stakes
- 1922 Golden Myth

YORK
Gimcrack Stakes
- 1931 Miracle
- 1960 Test Case

Great Voltigeur Stakes
- 1950 Castle Rock

Sir Jack Jarvis was Top Trainer in 1939, 1951 and 1953.

INDEX

151

Blue Train, 79
Bois Rousell, 86
Bongrace, 49-50, 52, 125
Borealis, 123-4
Botticelli, 79
Boussac, M. M., 77, 131
Boyd-Rochfort, Cecil, 57, 60
Brabazon, 14
Bray Melody, 133
Breasley, Scobie, 91, 139
Brewer, Jack, 34
Britannia Stakes, 46, 72
Brocklebank, Rev., 55
Broconteur, 78-9
Brulette, 67
Buchan, 72
Bullock, Frank, 91
Bullough, Sir George, 38, 40-1, 54-5, 65
Butters, Frank, 95
Buzzard, The; *see* Bastard, The

Call Boy, 57, 86
Cambridgeshire, 16-18
Cameronian, 52, 80-1
Campanula, 40
Cannon, Mornington, 84
Carlow, Gwen, 76
Carney, Jimmy, 96
Carslake, Bernard, 90-1
Carter, Frank, 66
Cecil, 63
Celiba, 71
Cesarewitch, 12, 37, 81
Challenge, 58, 78-9
Challenge Stakes, 121
Champion Stakes, 44, 49, 127-8
Charles, Sir James, 106
Charlottown, 74, 138-9
Cheltenham Gold Cup, 46
Chester Cup, 133
Chester Vase, 74, 80, 137
Childs, Joe, 61
Christmas Daisy, 17
Churchill Stakes, 39-40, 67, 133
Cheveley Park Stakes, 135
Cicero, 9
Cillas, 79
Cloncarrig, 63-4
Colling, George, 87
Colling, Mrs., 87

Collis-Browne, Monty, 55-6, 65-6, 144-6
Colombo, 59
Column Produce Stakes, 57, 123
Cononach, 57
Cook, Paul, 138-9
Cooke, Sir William, 36-8, 40
Cork and Orrery Stakes, 64, 128
Coronation Cup, 124, 127, 132
Coronation Stakes, 60, 65, 136
Court Line, 55
Court Martial, 121
Craganour, 86, 88-9
Craven Stakes, 44, 80
Creosote, 144
Crepello, 66
Cripps, Jerry, 35
Cumberland Lodge Stakes, 132
Cunliffe, A. P., 16
Cunliffe-Owen, Sir Hugo, 57
Cyllene, 9-10, 43, 98

Dalmeny, Lord, 42-3, 45, 50, 53, 71; *see also* Rosebery, 6th Earl of
Dante, 121, 130
Darling, Fred, 20, 75, 95
Dark Donald, 29
Dastur, 82
Davy, Captain, 36
Dawson, John, 26
Day Comet, 88
Day, Reg, 34
Daytona, 40, 65
de Mestre, Mr., 31
de Rothschild, Leopold, 11, 25-6
Dee Stakes, 132
Derby, 9-12, 23, 27, 39, 42-4, 52, 57, 59, 64, 67, 72-6, 79-80, 82, 84-8, 92, 95-7, 100-1, 103, 122-3, 126-7, 130-1, 136-9, 141, 145
Derby Cup, 19
Derby, 17th Earl of, 51, 58, 73, 94, 123, 125
Devizes, 36-7, 39-40
Dewhurst Stakes, 137
Dexter, Ted, 143
Dhoti, 74
Dialogue, 141
Dictaway, 129
Diomedes, 69
Donatello II, 66, 137

152

Doncaster Cup, 36, 49, 56, 63, 67, 132
Donoghue, Steve, 49, 86, 92, 104, 111, 115-17
Double, Percy, 28, 33, 43, 76, 141-2
Druids Lodge, 16-18
Duleepsinjhi, K. S., 143
Duller, George, 88
Duller, 'Hoppy', 88-9
Dundas, Lord George, 86
Dunlin, 144
Dunn, Tommy, 24
Dunnottar, 32
Durham, 3rd Earl of, 32

Earl of Sefton's Plate, 15
Earl, Walter, 32, 52
Easter, 22-3
Eastern Emperor, 132-3
Eastern Monarch, 40-1
Easton, 59
Eclipse Stakes, 39, 57-8, 77, 81-2, 86
Edmunds, Mr., 45
Eider, 89
Elizabeth II, Queen, 145-6
Ellangowan, 43-6, 51, 72
Ellesmere House, 28-9
Ellesmere, 4th Earl of, 56
Elliott, Charlie, 38-9, 44, 47, 49, 57-8, 86, 133
Enfield, 63
Eremon, 90
Esmond, Edmund, 66-8, 75, 82
Ezra, Sir Edward, 66

Faerie Queen, 65
Fair Judgement, 69
Fairstone, 74
Fairway, 33, 40, 50, 58, 72-3, 75, 98, 125, 128
Falcon, Archie, 38-9
Fallon, Jack, 16
Falmouth Stakes, 136
Fancy Free, 64, 71-2
Fearless Fox, 61-3, 133
Felstead, 57-8, 72
Fiddlededee, 54
Figaro, 69-70
Fighting Ship, 137
Firdaussi, 67, 82

Flamboyant, 56
Flamenco, 59-61
Flamingo, 56-9, 128
Flapper, 72
Florizel II, 21
Flyon, 59, 78
Forester, Captain Frank, 16
Fox Cub, 75
Fox, Freddy, 39, 49
Fox, Sir John, 46
Foxbrough II, 73
Foxcroft, 60-1
Foxhunter, 67
Foxlair II, 78-9
Foxlaw, 50, 61, 67
Free Handicap, 82, 134-5, 138
Freebooter, 64
Freemason Lodge, 24
French Derby, 66, 77, 79
French Gold Cup, 66
French One Thousand Guineas, 129
Fulbourne Stakes, 57
Full Sail, 72

Gainsborough, 98
Gainsborough Lass, 65
Garden Path, 123
General Gordon, 74, 136-7
George, Frederick, 27
George V, King, 11
Gerber, J. S., 135
Gibson, Cyril, 142
Gibson, G. C., 143
Gilles de Retz, 122
Gilpin, Victor, 82
Gimcrack Stakes, 66, 82
Glanely, Lord,, 38, 59, 143
Glasgow, 5th Earl of, 11
Glen Loan, 77
Glenister, Mr. and Mrs. M., 87-8
Glommen, 49-50
Godding, James, 10-11
Gold Vase, 39-40, 61-3, 86
Golden Cloud, 122
Golden Lily, 38
Golden Martlet, 64
Golden Myth, 38-40, 61-3, 86
Golden Orb, 36
Golden Seal, 61
Golden Suprose, 61

153

Goldhill, Sol, 32-3
Good Brandy, 135
Good, Meyrick, 122
Goodwood Cup, 50, 56, 63, 67-8, 86, 133
Gordon, Charles, 69
Gordon-Smith, Sir Allan, 61-4, 74
Gordon-Watson, Mrs. Michael, 69
Gorton, John, 91, 140
Gough, Captain G. P., 57
Grand National, 10, 22, 46, 63, 90
Grand Prix de Paris, 10, 66, 77-8, 120
Grant, Lady Sybil, 81
Gray, Colonel Douglas, 134
Grayson, Admiral, 113
Great Midland Breeders Plate, 72
Great Nephew, 129, 136-8
Great Sport, 89
Great Surrey Handicap, 96
Green Lodge, 12
Green, Sol, 33
Greenham Stakes, 96
Greenwood, George, 76
Griffiths, Major Osmund, 84-5
Griggs, Billy, 16
Groat, 46
Growing Confidence, 123
Gunn, Arthur, 54
Gustavus, 9

Hackler's Pride, 16-19
Hall, Sam, 144
Hallick, Johnny, 31
Halsey, Sir William, 54
Hamilton, 13th Duke of, 63
Happy Landing, 123
Happy Laughter, 66, 122, 133-6
Hardwicke Stakes, 10
Harewood, 5th Earl of, 95
Harewood, 7th Earl of, 95
Hartigan, Frank, 43
Hartley, Brigadier B. C., 145
Harvey, Wilfred, 81
Hastings Stakes, 132
Hastings, Aubrey, 22
Hastings, Sir Patrick, 63
Hastings-Bass, Peter, 22
Hatzfield, Prince, 22
Haulfryn, 63
Heliopolis, 73, 75

Herringbone, 50, 125-6
Heverswood, 69
Higgs, Billy, 15
High Table, 127
Hippius, 127-8
Hislop, John, 63
Historic, 124
Hobbs, Bruce, 90
Hobbs, Sir Jack, 140
Hobgoblin, 44
Hogg, Tommy, 94
Holliday, Major Lionel, 72
Honey Buzzard, 59-60, 128
Honeylight, 129
Honeyway, 33, 59, 123, 128-9, 131, 136
Horserace Totalisator Board, 144
Horus, 58
Hotweed, 66
Houldsworth, J. H., 12
Howard de Walden, 8th Baron, 65, 144
Howard de Walden, 9th Baron, 65, 144
Huggins, John, 96
Hulme, Mr., 47
Hulton, Sir Edward, 47, 71
Hunters Moon, 51-2
Hurry On, 46, 122
Hutchinson, Ron, 91
Hyperides, 81, 127-8
Hyperion, 98, 127, 130-2, 141

Imperial Produce Stakes, 73
Iona, 131
Irish National Stud, 64, 121-2, 134
Irish Two Thousand Guineas, 122
Irish St. Leger, 122
Irish, Mr., 101, 103-5, 112
Isinglass, 10, 78
Isleham Plate, 122

Jarvis, Sir Adrian, 66, 134
Jarvis, Basil, 12-13, 25, 44, 100-19
Jarvis, Ethel, 26-7, 69, 123, 141, 146
Jarvis, Sir John, 64-6, 120
Jarvis, Vivien, 27, 141, 145
Jarvis, William, 9-10, 12-13, 15-17, 20-1, 23, 25, 28, 34, 36, 43, 146
Jarvis, Mrs. William, 10, 12-13

154

155

Ravensbury, 9-10
Rawson, Mr., 35
Ray, 15
Reiff, Johnny, 85, 88-9, 97
Reiff, Lester, 85, 97
Reigh Count, 83
Reynard Volant, 63
Ribbon, 50, 77, 81, 99, 125-7
Richards, Gordon, 57-8, 90, 123, 133
Richardson, Sir Lewis, 69
Rickaby, Bill, 29, 62, 92, 132, 135-6
Rickaby, Fred, 29
Right Noble, 138
Robins, Tommy, 37
Robinson, Sir John, 57, 59
Rock Sand, 100
Rogotsky, 10
Romer, 19
Rose, C. D., 10
Rosebery, 5th Earl of, 7, 39-40,
    42-6, 48-50, 52-3, 81, 85
Rosebery, 6th Earl of (formerly
    Lord Dalmeny q.v.), 7-8, 46, 59,
    65, 67, 71-4, 76-7, 79-83, 97, 99,
    120, 122-7, 130-1, 137, 144
Rosebery, Lady, 123-4
Rous Plate, 47
Rous, Admiral, 13
Royal Charger, 64-5, 120-2, 133-4
Royal Dancer, 82
Royal Danieli, 90
Royal Forest, 87
Royal Lodge Stakes, 127
Royal Minstrel, 57
Royal Tan, 46
Royal, H.R.H. Princess, 137
Rush, E. C., 81
Ryan, James, 12
Ryan, Mrs., 26

Sadler, Alf, 23-4
Saffron Tartan, 46
St. David's, 1st Viscount, 67
St. James's Palace Stakes, 44, 57,
    59-61, 65
St. Leger, 10, 50, 58, 61, 67, 75, 77,
    79, 81-3, 100, 103, 120, 122, 124,
    126-7, 131, 139
St. Puckle, 137
Sande, Mr., 116
Sandwich, 80-1, 92

Sandwich Stud, 73, 81, 120
Sans Peine, 68
Sansovino, 44, 57, 80
Scottish Derby, 65
Scottish Union, 77
Scuttle, 11
Sea Bequest, 69
Sea Charger, 122
Sefton, 7th Earl of, 55
Select Stakes, 40
Selsey Stakes, 82
Shahpoor, 127
Shantung, 80
Sherwood, Bob, 16, 28, 34
Shogun, 88
Shrubb, Alfred, 24
Shy Lad, 20
Sigiri, 82
Signorinetta, 39
Silver Spray, 92
Sim, Sir Alexander, 144
Simms, Mr., 85
Sinclair, Mr., 109
Sir Ivor, 122
Skye, 131
Sloan, Tod, 85
Smirke, Charlie, 92
Smith, Doug, 92
Smith, Eph, 59, 62, 73, 75, 77-8, 92,
    121, 123-4
Smith, Lady Helen, 124
Snap, 97-8
Solario, 66, 120
Son-In-Law, 47, 51, 61
Souepi, 86, 133
Spear, 'Daddy', 29-31, 37
Spion Kop, 49-50
Sporting Life, 60, 122
Spring Stakes, 57
Springtime, 72
Stanley, Lord, 15
Starflower, 35
Stedall, A., 23-4
Stefan the Great, 71-2, 75
Stern, George, 89-90
Stewards Cup, 17, 64, 96
Stollery, Mr., 55
Straight Deal, 126
Straitlace, 47-8, 67
Stubbs, Jack, 140-1
Stud Produce Stakes, 133

157